CW00403538

CONTENTS

INTRODUCTION

The Key Principles VOL 31

G olf is a sport that's often perceived as being difficult and requiring much skill, but professional players and instructors know there are certain clear solutions that will greatly benefit the game of any player.

This guide dives into those solutions, so you the Golfer can identify, and improve problem areas in both your long and short game.
In this book, PGA teaching pros take you step-by-step through each solution, explaining in detail how to apply each one to the improvement of your game... with insightful suggestions, drills, and helpful photos/illustrations.

Golf is a challenging sport that can be played by people of all ages and abilities, but the golf swing can be tough to master. It is normal to have some aspect of your swing that needs work, nearly everyone does. Just by making a few adjustments, you can make significant changes to your swing path, lengthen or strengthen your drive, improve shot accuracy, and so much more.

◆ ◆ ◆

ACKNOWLEDGMENTS

Thomas Golf Inc.

thomasgolf.com

"The Most Accurate Clubs On Earth!" Premium Golf Equipment with Patented Shot Accuracy Technology and Guaranteed Custom Fitting and Performance.

golf-info-guide.com

Valuable Video Content

If you rather learn about the game through video rather than written content? No problem! Golf-Info-Guide.com has a wide range of videos (over 10,000) for you to view.

CHAPTER 1: BEFORE EVERY SHOT

Proper aim and body alignment lead to a good swing path.

People often forget, golf is a target game; and like any target game, aiming to the target is an essential first step. Your initial setup can give your mind and body the ability to swing freely in a correct swing path, free from the mechanical distractions and complications brought into the swing by misaligned body positions.

Visualize your target line, then align your body to that line. Here's how...

First, stand behind your ball and pick a small intermediate target on your target line

Then address the golf ball with your feet, hips, shoulders, and eyes parallel to that target line. You'll be surprised at what a huge impact this simple fundamental can have on shot performance.

Align your body (and club) properly, and let your golf swing flow.

By properly aiming your body along your target line, you increase the likelihood of a mechanically correct and free-flowing swing. When your feet, hips, shoulders, eyes, and club are not aligned with each other (or with the target), they conflict with each other and cause all sorts of problems with your swing and ball flight.

So go out there and AIM... ALIGN... SWING

Getting better at golf usually comes down to the small details. There isn't anything glamorous about working on your body alignment, but it can go a long way toward helping you play your best golf. Getting this fundamental correct requires patience on the driving range to work through the pre-shot process time after time until you have it down perfectly. Don't be tempted to make radical changes to your swing that might not even be necessary in the first place. Work hard on getting your body alignment correct before every shot to see quick and powerful results on the course.

Consistent Golf Starts with Proper Body Alignment before Every Shot

Aiming your golf shots is about more than just pointing the clubface at the target. Of course, the clubface is an important part of the equation, but the rest of your body needs to also be properly aligned in order to achieve a successful outcome. Poor body alignment can lead to bad golf shots even if the rest of your swing is perfectly executed. Take the time on the practice range to learn how to correctly align your body prior to every shot and you will be rewarded with improved performance on the course.

If you feel like you consistently make good swings throughout your rounds of golf – and yet your results aren't living up to your expectations – there is a good chance that poor body alignment is to blame. Many amateur golfers make mistakes while taking their stance and don't even know it. Misalignment of your feet, hips, or shoulders can all play a role in leading you to hit a bad shot. Don't automatically blame your swing when the ball goes in the wrong direction, as there is a chance the error occurred before the club was ever put into motion.

Learning how to align your body correctly is all about discipline. You need to have the discipline to work through the same set of steps before each and every shot in order to consistently achieve proper alignment. One of the reasons that it is so important to have a pre-shot routine in your game is to encourage correct alignment. If you were to just wander up to your ball and take a stance with no specific plan in place, you would most likely be aligned incorrectly. Golf is hard enough when you do everything right – don't add poor alignment to the list of challenges that you have to overcome.

It can actually be exciting to work on correcting your body alignment because you stand to make instant improvements to your game by fixing any pre-shot mistakes that you are making. Corrections to your swing itself can take weeks or months to actually begin benefiting you on the course. However, with something like body alignment, you can start to hit better shots and lower scores in your very next round. That opportunity alone should be enough to motivate you to get out to the practice range for a session dedicated to body alignment.

All of the instruction below is based on a right-handed golfer. If you play golf left-handed, please be sure to reverse the directions in order to apply them correctly to your game.

Railroad Alignment

Your body and the clubface need to be working together in order to create correct alignment prior to a shot. However, that does not mean that they should be aligned at the same target. If you have your body and the club pointed in exactly the same direction, you will be setting yourself up for failure. Instead, you should use the image of railroad tracks to create perfect alignment in your address position each and every time.

What do railroad tracks have to do with playing good golf? Railroad tracks run parallel to each other and never cross. This is exactly how you should be trying to align your body and the clubface at address. The line created between the clubface and your target, and the line created by your feet when you take your stance, should be parallel to each other. If those lines cross, you are setting your body up in a position that is going to make it difficult to successfully hit the ball at your target. Parallel lines should always be your goal when hitting a standard shot (you might break this rule occasionally to hit a 'specialty' shot like a big hook or slice to get out of trouble).

Make sure you take time to get this image perfectly clear in your head. If you are having trouble picturing the two lines, try the following drill –

On the practice range, pick out a target that is 100 yards or so away from where you are standing. Take an extra club out of your bag, and place it on the ground so that the end of the grip is just in front of the ball and the shaft of the club is pointing at the target you have selected.

Next, take your stance as if you were going to hit a shot at the target (don't actually hit the shot). Once you are happy with your stance, take the club you are holding and place it on the ground so that the shaft is touching the toe of both of your shoes.

Step back and look at the two clubs that you have laid on the ground. If you have taken your stance correctly, these two clubs should be parallel, just like railroad tracks. If the lines created by these clubs would cross out in front of you, something has gone wrong with your address position.

By far, the most common mistake that amateur golfers make is to align their feet toward the target, instead of parallel to the left of the target. When this happens, the body is aligned 'across' the correct line, and an over-the-top swing is usually the result. Many players who struggle with a slice could greatly improve their ball flight simply by aligning their bodies correctly at the address.

The concept of railroad tracks in your alignment is one that can lead to great improvement in your game. While it is a simple idea, this mental image will help you place your feet on the proper line so that your body doesn't get in the way of what you are trying to do with the club. While you are practicing your swing on the driving range, try placing a couple of clubs down on the ground parallel to each other for a guide. It shouldn't take long before you get comfortable with the idea of aligning your body parallel to the left of the target line. Even without making a single change to the mechanics of your swing, you can quickly start to hit better shots by using the mental image of railroad tracks to guide your alignment.

Make Sure All Parts of Your Body Are Working Together

Most golfers will check on their body alignment by looking down at their feet prior to starting a swing. While your feet are a good place to start, there are actually other parts of your body that you need to make sure are properly aligned as well. Specifically, it is important to check that your hips and your shoulders are placed along a line that is in concert with the line your feet have created. Ideally, all three of these 'lines' (feet, hips, and shoulders) will be pointing in the same direction – on a line that is parallel left of your target line.

For some golfers, this will come naturally. Some players are simply able to take a stance and have all of these lines match up perfectly at address time after time. Not everyone is so lucky, however. If you have trouble with this important fundamental, you will need to practice taking a square stance on the driving range so that you are able to duplicate that quality stance out on the course. Try using the following process to put your body into a perfect pre-shot position.

On the driving range, place two clubs down on the ground – one to indicate the target line that you are going to use for the shot, and one that is parallel left of the target line which you can use to align your feet. With those two clubs placed on the ground, take your stance, and prepare as if you were going to hit a shot.

Once in your stance, take the club that you are holding and place it across your waist so that the shaft of the club is parallel with the ground. The idea is to have this club represent the direction that your hips are pointing at the address. Hold the club across your waist and look down at the line it has created. Does this line match up with the club that is on the ground to guide your feet? If it does, you will know that your hips are properly positioned. If not, make the necessary adjustment to your stance until your hips are aligned in the same direction as your feet.

Next, repeat this process for your shoulders. Place the club across the front of your shoulders and make sure that it matches up with the direction of your feet and your hips. Once you have all three of these lines matched up nicely in your stance, go ahead and hit a shot down the range. Hopefully, your improved alignment will lead to more accuracy once the ball is actually struck.

You can use this drill as often as you would like on the driving range – even before every shot that you hit. Make it a habit to work through this process of checking your alignment until you are confident that your feet, hips, and shoulders are all working together nicely in your stance.

For some people, the above drill might not be enough to sort out misalignment issues. If you are still having trouble with correct body alignment after trying the drill, you may need to use video in order to correct your problems. Ask a friend to record a video of your swing so that you can see your body alignment from another perspective. To get the most-useful video, ask your friend to stand several feet behind you on an extension of the target line.

When you watch the video, look closely at the points that have been highlighted above – specifically, look for your target line and your foot line to be parallel to one another. Also, make sure that the lines formed by your feet, hips, and shoulders are all matching up nicely. Once you see yourself on video, it should become clear what adjustments need to be made in order to get your body alignment on track.

Everything is Based on
Your Target Line

You can't get into a good stance if you don't have a clear target for each shot – it is just that simple. Picking a target is one of the most overlooked fundamentals in golf. Many players simply walk up to the ball and aim at the middle of the fairway or at the flag without really giving it much thought. Instead, you should be working hard to pick a very specific target that plays to your strengths and will keep your ball out of trouble. Once you have picked that target, the job of getting your body aligned correctly becomes a whole lot easier.

As you approach any golf shot, the first thing you should do is look for potential trouble that lies ahead. This trouble could be a bunker or some deep rough, or it could be something more serious like a water hazard or out of bounds markers. Naturally, your goal should be to keep your ball out of trouble and in a good position throughout the round. Even if you don't hit the ball right next to the hole, staying away from the trouble will give you a chance to shoot a good score at the end of the day. Before you pick a club or even get your yardage, take a moment to select a specific target for the shot at hand.

After that target has been chosen, you can then move on to your other preparations such as finding yardage and picking the right club. However, while you are getting ready to hit the shot, never lose track of the target you are going to use. Golf is a target-based game, so the targets that you chose during a round are going to go a long way toward determining your success or failure.

With all other pre-shot work completed, you will step up to the ball and prepare to swing. This is when body alignment comes into play. Before setting your body into position, your first move should always be to place the club behind the ball. Set the clubhead down behind the ball and aim the face of the club perfectly at your target before doing anything else. Only when you are satisfied that the clubface is aimed correctly should you move on to getting your body in position.

Start by getting your feet set on a line that is parallel to your target line (don't forget about the railroad tracks). After your feet are settled, make a quick check of your hips and shoulders to be sure that they are in the right position as well. With your body correctly positioned, you can take one last look up at the target prior to starting your swing.

After reading through all of those steps that are required to get set for a shot, you might feel like you are going to have to spend five minutes just getting your body ready to swing. That is not the case. The pace of play is important in golf, so it is critical that you learn how to work through the process above in just a few quick seconds. The key is practice.

You should put yourself through plenty of repetitions of this process on the driving range so that you are able to repeat it automatically when you are playing on the course. Don't just mindlessly hit balls on the range and hope to get better – instead, go through your routine before hitting each shot so you can actually see a benefit from your practice. Rehearse your pre-shot routine and body positioning prior to all of your driving range shots and you will hardly have to think about the process once you get to the course.

Troubleshooting Your Body Alignment

Hopefully, the instruction above will allow you to quickly correct anybody's alignment issues that you have in your game. However, even if you are able to correct them for the time being, there is always a chance that new problems will come up later on down the line. Golf is a difficult game, and your mind is required to think of many different things all at the same time. Despite your best efforts, you may find that your body alignment gets off track at some point in the future. If that should happen, use the following troubleshooting guide to fix your mistakes.

The tips below are based on the ball flights that are giving you trouble. Find the ball flight that is currently causing problems in your game and make the appropriate correction as soon as possible.

Pulled shots. If you are pulling the ball to the left on a consistent basis, there is a chance that your body is aimed to the right of the correct line. This is a common mistake for amateur golfers to make. When you line the clubface up correctly, but your feet are aimed too far right, you will most likely have an over the top move in the transition from backswing to downswing. That mistake, along with active hands through the hitting area, can lead to a shot that is pulled to the left immediately off the clubface.

Pushed shots. The opposite mistake, pushing the ball to the right, is caused by the opposite problem. Allowing your feet to be aligned too far left at address will promote an outside takeaway – leading to an inside-out downswing. Doing this while keeping your hands quiet through the hitting area is a common way to create a pushed shot.

Hooked shots. Hooking the ball quickly to the left is a difficult ball flight to play with on the course, and it can actually have the same cause as hitting a pushed shot. An open stance that is aligned too far left will put you in danger of hitting a hook – especially if you are a player who uses aggressive hands through impact.

Sliced shots. As you might suspect, hitting a slice can be a common result when the body is aligned too far to the right. Just like when you hit a pull, the club comes from the outside-in and swipes across the ball. If you don't roll your hands over to square the clubface on this path, the shot will have plenty of slice spin.

If you are hitting any of these four ball flights on a consistent basis, it is important that you first look to correct your body alignment before taking any other steps. It would be a terrible mistake to try rebuilding your entire swing from scratch when the only problem was a minor issue with your alignment. In golf, you always want to try the easiest fixes first, and only move on to bigger corrections when the basic changes don't solve the problem. Work on your alignment on the driving range and see if getting your body in the right position is able to bring your ball flight back to the center of the course. If correcting your body alignment doesn't solve the issue, you can then move on knowing that there is another problem in your swing which needs to be fixed.

CHAPTER 2: FIRE RIGHT SIDE

G olf telecasts often feature super-slow-motion frames of the golf club impacts the ball. You'll notice that the clubhead continues traveling down the target line for several inches past impact, which is common among all pros.

Many amateurs, on the other hand, hit the ball with a jabbing action, the clubhead popping up abruptly after contact. This is caused by a poor release, with the right-hand and forearm (for a right-hander) failing to rotate over the left properly. In addition to the right arm, the entire right side of the body must rotate around to the left on the downswing and follow-through.

To ingrain a powerful right-side rotation, try to keep the club-head moving directly down the target line as far as possible after impact. It may help to imagine pushing the club toward the target with your right arm, with the hips and shoulders turning through as well.

Remember, the ball isn't the swing's endpoint. Practice swinging through the ball with your right side and you'll enjoy increased distance and accuracy.

Chase Club Down the Line
to Fire the Right Side

On the most basic level, the golf swing is an athletic motion. While golfers are good at overcomplicating the process by thinking too much about specific mechanics and positions, the best players are able to push all of those thoughts to the side while they execute the swing. Just like any other sport, golf is best performed when the body is allowed to naturally react to the target. If you are able to refine your technique on the driving range and then use that technique on the course without conscious effort, you will be on the road toward playing your best golf.

Unfortunately, most golfers struggle with making the transition from the range to the course. On the range, it is okay for your mind to be filled with technical thoughts, because that is where you need to work on your mechanics. However, those thoughts need to be left behind when you reach the first tee. This is a hurdle that many golfers never manage to clear.

Among the many key parts of the golf swing that require freedom of motion is the firing of the right side through the ball. As you reach impact, the right side of your body should be moving aggressively through the shot to release the clubhead and maximize speed. When done correctly, the clubhead will 'chase' the ball down the line, which will increase your chances of hitting a straight shot. Your right side will continue on into a full finish, and you will be able to watch the ball as it soars through the air toward your target.

Of course, if you are thinking too much about your mechanics during the swing, your right side will never get a chance to release properly. Mechanical thoughts slow down your movements, and your right side will likely fail to fire in time when your head is clouded. Instead, you should be thinking only about being as athletic as possible. By the time you are on the course, it is too late to fix your swing mechanics anyway – so you might as well be as athletic as you can in an attempt to hit a quality shot.

Firing your right side through the ball is the final step in the process of hitting a golf shot that is both powerful and accurate. Everything that leads up to this point is setting the stage for an aggressive move of your right side through impact. All of your other swing mechanics will be wasted if you don't let your right side fire, so be sure to hold nothing back once the club is making its way down toward the ball.

All of the instruction below is based on a right-handed golfer. If you happen to play left-handed, please reverse the directions as necessary.

It All Starts with Great Balance

The golf swing is not a single movement – rather, it is a combination of movements that culminate in the club being delivered to the back of the ball. While the best players in the world make the swing look like it is all one piece, the reality is quite different. Each piece of the swing builds on the one before, and you can only hit good shots once all of the pieces are working together beautifully.

With that in mind, a great balance is the first piece of the puzzle that needs to fall into place. If you are off-balance during your golf swing, you will have a hard time allowing your right side to fire through the shot. Many amateur golfers start the down-swing off balance, and they are never able to recover. Right from the start of the swing, the balance should be one of your main objectives.

Following are three keys to keeping your balance throughout the golf swing.

Staying within yourself. The biggest cause of poor balance in the golf swing is simply trying to swing too hard. This is an error that many amateur golfers are guilty of, and it is one that can wreck an otherwise sound motion. There is no need to swing extra-hard when hitting golf shots – the goal is accuracy, not distance.

Every golfer would love to hit the ball a little bit farther, but that distance should never come at the expense of your control over the ball. Before every shot, be sure that you have plenty of clubs to cover the distance to your target. If you are feeling like you need to squeeze every possible yard out of your swing in order to reach the target, you are going to swing too hard and lose your balance. Just by picking the right club for each shot, you can make it much easier to stay within yourself during the swing.

Avoiding the slide. Another common mistake is sliding to the right during the takeaway. As the club begins to move back away from the ball, you want to avoid shifting your weight onto your right foot. Instead, you should be nicely balanced while your body simply rotates around your center of gravity. In fact, throughout the entire backswing, there should be very little movement in your balance point. The backswing is all about rotation, and good rotation combined with great balance will set you up for an aggressive downswing that will enable you to fire your right side through the shot.

Starting on balance. It might seem obvious, but you need to start your swing on the balance if you hope to maintain that balance throughout the action. Pay attention to your address position and confirm that your weight is evenly distributed prior to starting the swing. Much of the success of your golf swing will be determined by the way you stand over the ball at address, so take the time to build a quality stance that will serve your well time and time again.

If you are able to arrive at the top of your backswing with a good balance, firing your right side during the downswing should be no problem at all. However, if you lose your balance somewhere during that backswing, the downswing will have very little chance of success. The best golfers in the world all pay close attention to their balance, and you should do the same.

Basic Fundamentals are Key

Once you have your balance under control, the next step is to check on the other 'fundamental' parts of your golf swing. These are keys that every golfer should pay attention to because they apply to all players regardless of their swing technique. Golf swings vary wildly from player to player, but some fundamentals apply across the board.

If you can put all three of the fundamentals below in place in your golf swing, you will have a much better chance of letting the club chase down the target line through impact.

Eyes on the ball. This is probably the first golf tip you ever received, and it is a good one. Watching the ball is incredibly important for a number of reasons. First, it is easier to hit something when you are looking at it, so your chances of hitting the sweet spot on the club go up when you keep your eyes on the ball.

Also, keeping your eyes down will help the mechanics of your swing. When the eyes come up early, the rest of your body has a tendency to lift up with the – meaning that you won't be able to keep the club moving down the target line as long as you would like. By keeping your eyes down, your head and shoulders will stay in the shot, and the club will be able to fire down the line perfectly.

Left foot flat on the ground. As you swing down toward the ball, you might feel the urge to push your weight up onto your toes as a way to get taller and swing harder. This is a bad idea. While it is okay for your right foot to roll up onto its toes, you want to keep your left foot flat on the ground.

This is a key point when it comes to allowing your right side to fire completely through the shot. If your left foot is moving up onto its toes, it will restrict and inhibit the release of your body in the downswing. Instead, leave that left foot flat on the ground and your body will be able to continue turning to the left all the way through impact.

Swing through the shot. The goal of your golf swing shouldn't be to just hit the ball – it should be to swing on through to a full, balanced finish. That might seem like a subtle difference, but it is important. If you are able to focus your mind on swinging all the way through to the finished position, you will be more likely to keep the club moving down the target line in the hitting area. Golfers who are only thinking about swinging down to the ball have a tendency to stop the motion of the swing prematurely – meaning they don't fire their right side completely, and their shots lack power and control. Prior to every swing, picture yourself posing in a balanced finish position as you watch the ball soar through the air.

There is nothing terribly difficult about the three fundamentals above. Each of those points is relatively easy to achieve, but they can do powerful things for your golf swing. One by one, work on each of the three points on the driving range until you can bring them all together in a cohesive motion. Once these fundamentals are present in each golf swing that you make, you will be most of the way toward your goal of firing the right side successfully through the ball.

A Powerful Drill

Golf swing drills are a great way to learn new techniques. While it might be fun to simply stand on the driving range and hit shot after shot with your regular swing, you probably aren't going to get much better that way. Instead, you should use drills to teach yourself skills that can be applied when you go back to your regular full swing. When it comes to firing the right side through the shot, there is one drill specifically that can help you make great progress.

To complete this drill, follow the simple steps below.

Head to the driving range with your clubs and a bucket of golf balls. You can do the drill with a variety of clubs, so it is best to take your whole set with you, if possible.

Before starting, make sure to warm your body up with a few light stretches and some practice swings. You don't want to exert your body too much right off the bat, so take a few moments to get warmed up before jumping into the drill.

When you are ready, pull out one of your short irons from the bag. It is best to start with a short iron, and then move on to longer clubs once you get the hang of the drill.

To start, you are only going to be swinging with your right-hand on the club – and you won't be hitting a ball. Take your stance as you normally would prior to a regular shot, but drop your left-hand off of the grip before continuing.

With only your right-hand on the grip of the club, make a full one-handed swing that leads to a balanced finish. The focus during this practice swing should be on using your right-hand to aggressively move the club through the hitting area. Since your left arm isn't even holding on to the club, you will have no choice but to fire your right side in the downswing. Also, without your left-hand to pull the club off of the target line, it should be easy to chase the clubhead toward the target.

Make five consecutive practice swings using just your right-hand. After five swings, place a ball down in front of you and put your left-hand back on the club. You are going to hit this shot with your regular swing, but remember the feeling you had during the one-handed swings. Use your right side throughout the downswing, and chase the clubhead along the target line for as far as possible. Hit three total shots while focusing on these swing keys.

After three shots with both hands on the club, go back to making right-hand-only practice swings without hitting a ball. Again, you are going to take five practice swings, followed by hitting three shots with both hands.

You can go back and forth between one-handed practice swings and two-handed shots for as long as you would like. After you get comfortable using a short club for this drill, feel free to move up to some of your longer clubs.

The key to this drill is going back and forth between the two different types of swings. The feelings that you get from the one-handed practice swings will be powerful, and they will lead you into better habits with your regular swing. However, it takes repetition to ingrain these new mechanics into your swing. For that reason, work on moving back and forth between both types of swings until you can feel your right side working effectively even when you have two hands on the club.

Since this drill isn't too technical, it is a good one to use prior to a round. While warming up for your round, make a few practice swings using just your right-hand to remind yourself of how you want to use your right side during the swing. You don't even need to think consciously about your technique while using this drill – just make the swings and your body will feel the right movements.

Troubleshooting

Even after putting in plenty of practice time on the range, you might find that you are still having a little trouble with using your right side effectively. If you haven't gotten much help from your right side over the years on the golf course, this will be a big change – and big changes rarely come easy in golf. Even if you are on the right track, there are almost inevitably going to be bumps along the way. It is important that you don't give up on this part of the swing just because you have some trouble at first. Stick with the goal of firing your right side through your shots, and keep searching until you find the answers to your problems.

To help locate those answers, review the troubleshooting advice below.

Hitting the ball fat. It is common for players who are trying to use their right side more in the swing to start hitting the ball fat from the fairway. A fat shot is one where you hit the turf before the ball, and the ball will then come up short of the target. Most likely, this is happening because your lower body is not doing its job early in the downswing.

As you transition from backswing to downswing, your lower body should be rotating left and pulling the rest of your body into action. If that doesn't happen properly, you won't be in a position to fire your right side through the shot. Instead, you will be stuck on your right foot, and the club will enter the turf too far behind the ball. Engage your lower body earlier in the downswing to get your body moving left and the club should quickly start to find the ball first, instead of the turf.

Hitting thin shots. This is the opposite of hitting fat shots, as a thin shot results when you hit the ball too low on the clubface. The cause in this case is usually your left shoulder lifting up and out of the shot. While firing your right side through the ball, you may be tempted to lift up with your left side to make room for the swing.

This is an unnecessary move and one that will make it hard to find solid contact. To alleviate this mistake, go back to your fundamentals and make sure you are keeping your eyes down on the ball through impact. As long as you watch the ball until it leaves the clubface, you should be able to keep your left side down into the shot nicely.

Pulling the ball left. Even if you make solid contact, you might not always send the ball flying down your target line. If you notice that you are missing too many of your shots to the left, there is a good chance that you aren't finishing the backswing completely. In an effort to get started firing your right side down toward the ball, you may be cutting off your backswing before it is finished. When that happens, your lower body won't be able to clear properly, and the clubface may be closed at impact. Fixing this problem comes down to a better tempo. Give the club time to complete the backswing by slowing down your takeaway and focusing on maintaining an even rhythm from start to finish.

Firing your right side through the ball is a powerful way to hit accurate golf shots, but it is a skill that can take some time to master. It is necessary for most players to spend plenty of time on the practice range working on their swing fundamentals before they will be able to chase the club down the target line properly. Once you do make these improvements to your swing, you will quickly notice how the ball is jumping off your club with more speed than ever before. The golfer who can use their right side effectively has a big advantage in the competition, so it is worth your time and effort to learn this important part of the swing.

CHAPTER 3: DISTANCE
FROM BALL AT SETUP

I f you've played golf for any length of time, you've probably established an address position where you stand at a comfortable distance from the ball. But comfortable doesn't necessarily mean correct.

How far you stand from the ball is a critical fundamental. Heel-to-toe balance and swing plane are two factors partially determined by this single, simple element. In fact, you may be standing too close or too far from the ball without even knowing it, because you've grown accustomed to playing from this position.

Here's an easy trick to test if you're the right distance, and to guide you toward fixing the issue if you're not:

Address a golf ball in your normal position. Any club will work, driver through lob wedge.

Carefully place the butt of the grip on your left leg while retaining your address posture. Make sure not to change the position of the clubhead or lock your knees.

The club should touch your left leg about two inches above the kneecap. (A little higher if you tend to grip down more than an inch.)

If it's considerably higher than two inches, you're probably standing too close to the ball. Lower than two inches and you're too far away.

If you've been missing shots left or right, making contact on the club's heel or toe, or hitting the ball fat or thin, merely adjusting your address position could be all the fix you need.

If you determine that an adjustment is in order, remember – the correct position will feel unnatural for a while, so practice it frequently until you're comfortable again.

Check Your Distance from the Golf Ball at Setup

Despite the fact that they are both swinging sports, baseball and golf don't actually have that much in common. The fundamentals for swinging a baseball bat are drastically different than those used to hit a golf ball, and obviously, the golf ball is sitting still while a baseball can be traveling in excess of 90 miles per hour. Both games are extremely popular throughout the United States and in much of the rest of the world, but they really are quite different.

One of the major differences between hitting a baseball and hitting a golf ball is that in golf, you can control how far away from the ball you stand while making your swing. Obviously, this is not an option in baseball. You get to decide where you stand in the batter's box, but ultimately it is up to the pitcher as to where the ball is going to be placed. As a hitter, you have to react to the ball as it is coming toward you and adjust your swing accordingly. Naturally, this makes hitting a baseball extremely challenging.

Thankfully, golfers don't have to worry about that problem. When you step up to the ball, you get to control exactly how far away you are standing. Having control over this element of the game means you can make basically the same swing each and every time – assuming you are successful in standing the same distance from the ball each time. One of the most important skills in golf is being able to setup up your shots in exactly the same manner, time after time. If you are a different distance from the ball prior to every shot throughout a round, it will be impossible to find consistency in your game.

The distance that you stand from the ball prior to making your swing is one of those fundamentals that you probably haven't given much thought up to this point. Most golfers are too busy worrying about things like grip and posture to concern themselves with their distance from the ball. However, your entire address position has a profound impact on the quality of your shots, and that includes the distance that you are standing from the ball while making your swing. If you can take the time to focus on this seemingly small element of the game, you can actually make major progress in the consistency of your ball-striking.

All of the instruction below is based on a right-handed golfer. If you play left-handed, please take a moment to reverse the directions as necessary.

Every Golfer is Unique

It would be easy if every golf needed to stand exactly the same distance from the ball. Of course, that is not the case. The correct distance for you to stand from the ball will be unique to you based on your height, stance, swing style, and much more. If you think you will just be able to copy the stance of another golfer and move on with your game, you are going to be disappointed in the results. No one swings the golf club in exactly the same way that you do, so you will need to build a stance that is designed to meet your needs.

The paragraph above should make it clear that you are not going to be able to use any kind of static measurement in order to determine the correct distance from the ball at address. You can't, for instance, decide that you are going to stand exactly 18" from the ball on each swing. For one thing, it would be difficult to measure out that distance while taking your stance.

Also, the distance that you stand from the ball changes with each different club in your bag because they are all a different length. Therefore, you actually have to have a stance for all 13 'swinging' clubs in the bag (not counting the putter). Obviously, these stances will be mostly the same, but they will vary a little bit in terms of the width of your stance and your distance from the ball.

Golf is largely a game about 'feel', and you are going to have to use your feelings when you are building a good stance. Rather than being able to precisely measure the distance that your feet are away from the golf ball before each shot, you are going to need to develop the ability to feel the correct positioning. When you stand over the ball, you should instantly know whether or not your feet are in the right place – and if they aren't in the right place, you should be able to quickly adjust in order to solve the problem. This still won't be developed overnight, but you will need to improve in this area if you wish to reach your goals on the course.

It is common for amateur golfers to resist the 'feel' elements of the game, instead of wanting specific directions as to how they should stand, swing, etc. Unfortunately, golf really doesn't work that way, and trying to formulate your game scientifically is a pursuit that is destined to fail. Instead, you need to trust your instincts and allow your natural ability to shine through. It is only when natural feelings are combined with practice and repetition that you will be able to truly see what you are capable of accomplishing.

The purpose of this section is to make one point perfectly clear – you are your own individual on the course, and everything that you do has to be tailored to your own golf swing. That includes how far you stand from the ball at address, along with a long list of other technical elements. Trying to copy other players is not going to help you play great golf. You can certainly learn little bits and pieces of the swing from other golfers, especially the pros, but in the end, you need to create your own swing from the ground up. When it comes to finding the right distance from the golf ball for your swing, don't worry about what others are doing – simply use some basic guidelines to find a spot that allows you to perform your best.

Find the Right Spot for You

As should be perfectly clear by this point, the goal when building your stance is to find the right address position for you personally. So how do you go about making that happen? The best way to find your own positioning in relation to the ball is to follow some general rules while also allowing your body to settle into a comfortable spot.

The 'rules' listed below aren't so many rules as they are guidelines. If you find yourself not exactly following one of these points because you are more comfortable making a small adjustment, that is no problem at all. In the end, the only thing that matters is the quality of your golf shots. If the stance you settle on allows you to hit great shots, then it is doing its job.

The first point that you need to understand is that your arms should be hanging freely from your shoulders at address. What does that have to do with the position of your feet? Everything. If you allow your arms to hang down naturally from your shoulders, and you then place your hands on the grip of the club, you will automatically know approximately how far to stand from the ball. Basically, your arms and the club itself will be telling your feet where to go.

This is why it is so important to take your stance in the right order. When you walk up to the ball, place the clubhead down behind the ball before doing anything else. With the clubhead in position, hold the grip steady with one hand while moving your feet into an 'approximate' stance. Note: this is not your final stance. You simply want to put your feet in a position that allows you to hang your arms down to your grip. Once your arms are hanging down, grab onto the grip of the club without forcing your arms either in closer to your body or out farther away.

Now that you are holding onto the club and the clubhead is behind the ball, the final step is to put your feet into position. Believe it or not, this last step should actually feel pretty easy because you are already in such a great spot with your arms.

Position your feet comfortably under your shoulders so that you are balanced and ready to make an athletic swing. There should be no sense of 'reaching' or being 'cramped' at the address – instead, you should feel totally comfortable and relaxed. When you are able to find these feelings at address, you will know yours have positioned your feet just right.

The beauty of using the method outlined above to take your stance is that it won't need to change based on the club that you are holding in your hand. You will be standing farther away from the ball at address with a driver compared to any of your irons simply because the driver is the longest club in your bag – but the process of taking your stance will be the same. Start with the clubhead resting behind the ball and build from there. When done correctly, you should be able to build a consistent stance that places your feet in a comfortable position prior to starting every swing.

Making Adjustments

Nothing about golf is simple. Just when you think you have figured out exactly how to take your stance in order to position yourself the correct distance from the ball, you start to realize that you can't use the exact same stance for every shot. Depending on the situation that you find yourself in on the course, and the kind of shot you are trying to hit, you will need to adjust your stance on the fly. Golf is not played on perfectly flat, evenly mowed pieces of land – rather, it is played on terrain that is often hilly, with various cuts of grass and even sand and water to get in the way. These are the elements that make golf so interesting, but they also make it complicated at the same time.

With all of that in mind, you are going to need to become adept at adjusting your stance on the go depending on the situation in front of you. If you are too stubborn to adjust and you simply use the same stance for every shot, you will never live up to your potential. The following are three basic ways in which you can adjust to create different shots or to deal with a challenging situation.

Closer to fade, farther to draw. When you are in your 'standard' position at address, you will produce a specific ball flight most of the time. For some golfers that will be a fade, for others it is a draw. While it doesn't really matter which shot you favor, it does matter that you can produce the same one over and over again. Predictable ball flights lead to good scores. But what happens when you want to change your ball flight to handle the layout of the hole in front of you?

If you generally hit a draw but the shot you are playing calls for a fade, how do you make that happen? One easy way to adjust your ball flight is to either move closer to the ball or to stand farther away, depending on the shot you want to hit. For most players, standing farther from the ball will encourage a draw pattern, while standing closer will make it easier to hit a fade. Of course, you are going to need to practice these adjustments on the driving range before you ever put them to use on the course.

Stand up tall in the rough. When you are playing a shot from relatively deep rough, you will want to stand up slightly taller in order to create a downward angle of attack. That downward angle is important if you hope to dig the ball out of the rough with any kind of authority. If you come into the ball from a flat angle, you will simply catch too much grass prior to hitting the ball – and your shot will fall well short of the target. As you adjust your stance to make yourself taller over the ball, you will also need to stand slightly closer in order to reach the ball effectively. With only those two minor adjustments – standing taller and slightly closer – you can dramatically improve your performance on shots played from the deep rough.

Get in close when the ball is below your feet. Playing a shot where the ball is sitting well below the level of your feet is one of the biggest challenges for golfers of all skill levels. It is hard to 'get down to the ball' on this kind of a lie, and many players will hit the ball thin as a result. If you do manage to get down to the ball, it is easy to turn it over and hit a quick hook as the heel of your club digs into the turf and shuts the face.

While nothing is going to make this an easy shot to play, it can be made slightly easier simply by standing closer to the ball than you would on a flat lie. Move your feet a few inches closer to the ball at address, while being sure to maintain a good posture. As you swing down, focus on keeping your weight over your feet (instead of allowing it to drift out over the ball). As long as you stay on balance and don't try to swing too hard, you should be able to strike decent shots from this awkward lie by standing closer to the ball.

The need for adjustments on the golf course is why it is so important to master your basic technique on the driving range before playing an actual round of golf. You need to become extremely comfortable with the process of building your 'stock' stance on the driving range. Once your normal stance has become comfortable and easy to build, you can then go onto the course and feel ready to adjust as necessary. Without that baseline stance to start from, however, you would be lost when it comes time to make adjustments.

Letting Your Feel Come Through

As mentioned earlier, golf is a game that should be largely about feeling while you are playing on the course. There is a time and a place to learn the technical elements of the game – and that place is on the driving range. You can certainly improve your overall performance by improving on your fundamentals, but technique alone will never enable you to get the ball into the hole on a regular basis. Instead, you have to know how to play the game, meaning you have to adjust to everything the golf course throws at you throughout an entire 18-hole round.

It is easy to become somewhat obsessed with the technical details of the golf swing while you are playing a round. For example, if you have been working on your distance from the ball on the range, you may find yourself looking down at your feet right before you hit a shot on the course, wondering if you are standing in the right place. If there is any doubt in your mind, you may fiddle with your stance a few times before you finally settle on an address position and begin your swing.

Obviously, this is not the best way to play golf. If you are thinking about a technical detail like how far you are standing from the ball, your mind isn't focused on the process of hitting your target. Golf requires both a clear focus and plenty of confidence in order to play well – and none of those things will be present in your game if you are distracted by small mechanical details. All of those thoughts should be left on the driving range so that you have plenty of brain space available to focus on the task at hand.

As you know, however, that is easier said than done. It is hard to separate your technical thoughts from the thoughts that you should be using on the course. That challenge becomes even greater if you hit a few poor shots because you will start to doubt your technique even if you have been hitting the ball great on the range. Once those technical doubts start clouding your mind on the course, you will face an uphill battle to get your round back on track.

So how do you avoid getting in your own head? Use a solid and predictable pre-shot routine. Having a routine will instantly give comfort to your mind, as you will feel much the same as you did when you were hitting balls on the range. Develop a pre-shot routine during your practice sessions and work on it just as much as you work on your swing itself. Your routine should include the steps necessary to take your stance, as well as every-thing you want to do just prior to making a swing. Nearly every professional golfer in the world uses some form of pre-shot rou-tine, and you just might be surprised at what a difference it can make in your game.

It is important to stand the right distance from the golf ball at address – but that 'right' distance will vary from player to player. Use the information contained in the content above to work on your own positioning at address, and you should see your ball-striking performance quickly begin to improve. Golf will never be easy, but standing in the right place time after time will make it just a little bit easier.

CHAPTER 4: CHIPPING TWO-TIERED GREENS

G reens with separate tiers or levels are the bane of many amateur golfers. That goes double when a chip shot must traverse one tier to reach a pin on the other, requiring a deft combination of judgment and touch.

Most two-tiered greens feature a lower level in front and a higher one in back, though they're sometimes configured side-to-side. When your ball is just off the lower section and the pin is on the upper half, you've got a couple of options:

Play a chip-and-run that flies low, lands on the bottom section, and rolls up to the top.

Hit a high-lofted shot that carries onto the top shelf and stops quickly.

The first option is generally much easier to execute since it doesn't require you to carry the ball at a precise distance with the height and spin to make it stop. When playing the chip-and-run, always remember your primary goal: to get the ball onto the same level as the flag. The last thing you want is to leave the ball short, on the bottom tier, leaving a long putt of the same difficulty. A less-lofted club, such as a mid-iron or hybrid, will produce a low chip with little spin and maximum roll.

When chipping from a higher level to a lower one, carrying the ball to the bottom tier isn't usually an option as you may be unable to keep it on the green. Therefore, you'll need to chip onto the top tier and let the ball trickle down the slope to the hole. The primary objective is the same as when chipping uphill – to get the ball onto the same section as the hole for a make-able putt – so be sure the ball reaches the edge of the top tier with enough speed to send it down the slope.

Chipping to a Two-Tiered Green

Playing a hole with a two-tiered green can present a challenge for a number of reasons. Obviously, if you find yourself on one tier and the hole is located on the other, you are going to have quite a difficult putt in front of you. Just managing to two-putt in such a situation is no easy feat. However, it is not only putting that is made more difficult by the presence of a tier in the middle of the green. Your chip shots are likely to be harder as well, and that is going to be the subject of the chapter to follow.

When chipping to a two-tiered green, you could face a variety of potential challenges. For instance, you could be on the high side of the tier, chipping down the slope toward the cup. This would make for a shot which is very difficult to control, and you might have trouble even keeping the ball on the green at all.

Or, on the other hand, you could be chipping up the slope to a hole that is cut just on top of the tier. In this case, you will need to make sure that you hit the ball hard enough to reach the top – but not so hard that the ball goes racing past the hole. As a third option, you might find yourself needing to chip across the side of the tier. This may be the most difficult position of all, as it can be extremely difficult to identify the proper landing spot to wind up with a good result.

To successfully navigate golf holes that feature two-tiered greens, there are a couple of things you'll need to consider. First, you will need to have a plan to keep your ball in the right position whenever possible. By avoiding tough spots around the green, you can make your life much easier when it comes to the short game.

Also, when you do wind up in a bad spot, you need to have a plan for how you are going to play these tricky chips. Even the best planning in the world can't keep your golf ball out of bad positions all the time, so a good player will know how to approach a difficult short game shot with confidence. Only when you have a smart game plan and the ability to get yourself out of trouble will you be able to reach your scoring potential.

All of the content below is based on a right-handed golfer. If you happen to play left-handed, please take a moment to reverse the directions as necessary.

Chipping Up the Slope

The first situation we are going to address is probably the easiest that we will cover, but it still has it's challenging. In this case, you are going to be chipping up the slope, playing your chip from the low side of the green up to a hole located on the top of a tier. Right away, we can see that you have the advantage of being in this position, in that you aren't going to have to worry too much about the shot getting away from you. With the tier available to help slow down the shot, it will be relatively easy to control your distance – especially when compared with the opposite situation of chipping down the hill.

With that said, you still need to pay attention first and foremost to the speed of the shot. Specifically, you want to make sure that the ball makes it all the way up the slope. You certainly don't want to see the ball rolling back down toward you after coming up short of the top of the tier. As long as you get somewhere up on the top, you should have at least a reasonable chance to make your putt and save your up and down.

So, how should you approach this shot? There are two main options, each of which is highlighted below.

Use spin to stop the shot. This is the aggressive option, and you are going to need a clean lie to make it work. If your ball is resting on the short grass and you feel like playing aggressively with this chip shot, you can hit the ball hard into the slope and use spin to bring it to a stop. This type of shot is played with a lofted wedge – usually, a sand wedge or lob wedge – and the ball will be placed near the middle of your stance.

Hit down on the ball firmly at impact, imparting as much spin as you can when sending the ball on its way. If you strike the shot nicely, the ball should bounce once or twice before coming to a quick stop. The idea here is to land the ball either into the slope or just before the slope. The bounces will take the ball up to the top, and it will then stop almost immediately.

Needless to say, this is an advanced technique that requires a steady nerve to execute under pressure. If you miss-hit this shot at all, the ball won't have much spin and it will probably bounce and roll well beyond the target. Or, if you don't carry the shot far enough in the air, the spin may cause the ball to stop before it reaches the top of the tier – and it will roll back down the slope. This is a shot that needs to be practiced extensively before it is put into action out on the links.

Use pace and slope to stop the ball. This other option is not going to use spin to bring the ball to a stop, but rather it will use the pace of the shot and the slope of the ground. Here, you are going to play a low running shot, often called a bump-and-run. While it will be easier to control this shot from a clean lie in the fairway, you can use it from the rough as well. The goal is to get the ball down onto the ground and rolling as quickly as possible.

Once the ball is on the ground, it will behave just like a putt the rest of the way. As long as you have judged the speed correctly, the ball will roll out toward the cup and come to rest, leaving you a short putt for your up and down. There is less risk involved in this method, but some golfers find it harder to control their distance precisely. Through plenty of practice, you should be able to determine which of these two options is going to be best for your game. Ideally, you will develop confidence in both of them, so you can pick from either option depending on the situation at hand.

If you have to chip to a two-tiered green, you usually want to be in the position of chipping up the slope. Of course, that is not a surprise, as you almost always want to be below the hole in the short game. Playing short shots uphill is easier than playing them downhill since it is not nearly as difficult to get the ball to stop.

Chipping Down the Slope

Moving on, we are now going to address the challenge of playing a chip shot down the slope to a lower tier. This is almost always going to be a tough shot, but there are some strategies you can use to give yourself a reasonable chance at success. The first thing you need to understand is that your expectations need to match the shot at hand. This is a tough shot, and you shouldn't be expected to navigate it perfectly. Leaving the ball right next to the cup would be quite an achievement, and you should be pretty happy with simply chipping the ball onto the right tier.

Just as we did in the previous section, we are going to highlight different options you can use when playing this type of shot. However, rather than the two options that we found when chipping up the slope, there are going to be three options at your disposal when going down the tier.

Bump-and-run down the hill. When the slope isn't too severe, you may be able to simply play a bump-and-run chip across the green, down the tier, and to the hole. It will always be a bit tricky to control the speed on this shot, but it is still the safest option on a relatively tame green. Of course, you'll want to be sure to apply enough speed to the shot to avoid leaving the ball on top of the tier. This is the first option you should consider, since it is the easiest to play, and it is also the best bet when you have a bad lie.

Use spin to stop the ball at the top of the tier. This is similar to the shot that we mentioned in the previous section, where you chip the ball into the slope and use slope to stop it quickly. In this case, you are going to again use spin, but you are going to land the ball on top and use the spin to take speed off the shot before it rolls down the slope. Basically, the shot should land on the high section of the green, bounce once or twice, almost come to rest, and then roll down the hill toward the hole.

You won't be surprised to learn that this is a difficult shot to pull off effectively. You are going to need a clean lie in order to get the spin you need, and your nerves need to be steady in order to strike the ball perfectly. Miss-hitting this shot will lead to a lack of spin, and the ball is going to travel way too fast as it goes down the hill. This is an option you should consider when the pin is located right at the base of the slope. If you pull it off correctly, the ball can trickle down the tier and come to rest much quicker than if you used the bump-and-run shot.

Carry the ball over the tier. The last option on our list just might be the most difficult. If you don't think you can stop the ball on the lower tier using either of the first two choices – which may be true if you are facing a particularly steep ridge – your only option may be to fly the ball all the way down to the lower section of the green. Needless to say, this is a very challenging shot. You have to clip the ball off the grass just perfectly to toss it high in the air without hitting it too far. You will need a good lie to attempt this kind of shot, with your ball either sitting on the fairway cut or just into the short rough.

Play the shot with your most-lofted club, and lay the face of that wedge open at the address to maximize the loft. Then, make a big swing and do your best to cut under the ball cleanly. When you pull it off, the ball will jump high up into the air, and land softly when it comes back down. If you manage to do all that and judge the distance right, you could be left with a brilliant result. Despite the potential for a great outcome, this is a shot that is best left as a last resort. It's hard to pull off, and it's never going to be consistent, even for a skilled golfer.

You have three main options at your disposal when chipping from the high side of the green down a tier, but none of them are all that attractive. This is a situation you would rather not deal with at all, since the chances of getting up and down are relatively low. Take some time during practice to work on these three kinds of shots and you will have all of them available to you on the course. Even if this situation is not a good one, you can make the best of it by picking the right shot and executing it properly.

Chipping Across the Slope

With chipping up the slope and chipping down the slope covered, the remaining situation to discuss is chipping across the side of the slope toward the hole. Depending on the severity of the slope, and the angle of your shot, this could be the toughest situation of all. There are multiple factors at play here, so you will have to think through the shot carefully before you decide how to proceed.

In this section, we can't really provide you with a list of different shots to use, because there are just so many different possibilities here. Instead, we have created a list of points to think about when facing this difficult shot.

Find a landing spot. This tip isn't exactly unique to chipping across a slope, since you should pick a landing spot for all of your short game shots. It is particularly important here since you need to figure out where the ball should land in relation to the slope in the middle of the green. Ideally, you will be able to avoid landing the ball right in the middle of the tier. You'll want to either land the ball below or above the tier, depending on the angle of the shot and the location of the hole.

Don't take on too much risk. The first goal you have in mind when playing this kind of shot should be to have the ball finish on the same level of the green as the hole. So, if the hole is on top of the tier, your ball needs to wind up on top of the tier, as well. Or, if the hole is on the bottom level, you'll need to make sure to keep your ball down below. With this in mind, pick a smart landing spot that is going to ensure you end up on the right level. If you cut it too close while trying to hit a perfect shot, you might end up on the wrong level, and you will have a particularly difficult putt as a result.

Think about your lie. If you have a good lie on short grass, you can consider using spin to your advantage. However, if the ball is sitting down in longer grass, spin isn't going to be an option. Take a moment to take a close look at your lie and decide how the grass around and under the ball is going to influence the outcome of your shot.

There isn't anything we can say here that is going to make this an easy shot. It's tough to play across a tier when chipping, as there is likely to be a lot of side-to-side breaks to deal with. When you do find this situation, remember that you need to play it safe and make sure to get your ball on the right tier first and foremost. Even if you don't hit a great shot, leaving your ball on the right tier can help you minimize the damage as you finish out the hole.

Strategy Points

In this last section, we are going to turn away from the topic of chip shots and talk about how to make good decisions on your approach shots. After all, if you can position your ball properly with the approach you hit into the green, you won't have to deal with the challenging chip shots that we have been talking about in this chapter.

The first thing you need to do is pick a club that is likely to leave your ball on the proper level. If the hole is cut in the back, make sure you take enough club to get up over the top of the ridge. Or, if the hole is cut in the front, use a club that is either going to land right next to the hole or come up just a bit short (unless there is a hazard short of the green to work about). Smart club selection is a big step in the right direction toward staying away from tricky spots around two-tiered greens.

Another key when hitting an approach shot to a two-tiered green is to take note of whether you would rather be on the left or right side of the green. If the green has any side-to-side tilt, you'll want to wind up on the low side, so you can make your next shot a little bit easier. Favor the low side when picking a target, and use a ball flight that it is going to make it more likely for you to wind up on that side, as well. Even if you don't place your approach shot in the perfect spot, finding the low side of the green is going to make your next shot much easier to handle.

Finally, you'll want to think about bringing your approach shots in low to a two-tiered green when the hole is cut in the back. A low approach shot is going to encourage some bounce and roll after the ball lands, and that is going to help you get all the way on top of the back tier. You don't have to use this strategy on every approach shot into a two-tiered green, but it is effective when the hole is cut toward the back of the putting surface.

If your favorite golf course features a number of two-tiered putting surfaces, you will want to have plenty of options at your disposal when you have to hit a chip shot from around one of these greens. The advice provided in this chapter should point you in the direction with regard to how you'll want to approach these kinds of shots. Of course, no part of your game is going to improve without practice, so spend some time learning how to play these shots in practice before using them on the course. Good luck!

CHAPTER 5: CHOKE UP

While it's true that using the entire length of a golf club produces longer shots, this also hinders control. Gripping down on the golf club an inch or more from the butt of the shaft – called "choking up" or "gripping down" -can greatly improve your accuracy.

Several prominent pros, including Anthony Kim and Sergio Garcia, choke up on almost every shot, even with the driver. Of course, they generate tremendous clubhead speed, so losing a few yards isn't a big deal.

In fact, choking up can actually help non-pros gain distance. How? Having better control of the club makes it easier to hit the sweet spot, negating the small loss in clubhead speed.

Choking up on iron shots can boost your greens-in-regulation percentage (GIR) – a great way to lower your scores. You'll make better contact, of course, and your misses won't sail as far off line. You may also achieve a lower ball flight, a big advantage in windy conditions.

Consider choking up on the golf club if you struggle with accuracy, or if the club feels difficult to control during the swing. Experiment by gripping the club at different lengths from the top until you feel comfortable and hit straighter, more solid shots.

Choke Up on the Club for Better Accuracy and Contact

Two of the most important elements of playing good golf are hitting accurate shots and making solid contact. In fact, those two things usually go hand in hand. When you hit the ball accurately, you are typically hitting it solid as well, as vice versa. Most golfers would love to add both accuracy and improved contact to their game because that combination will surely lead to lower scores.

Of course, just as with everything else in golf, it is not always easy to improve on these two crucial areas of your game. It takes plenty of hard work and practice to fine-tune your swing to the point where you can strike the ball cleanly – and hit it directly at your target – time after time. Even the best players in the world struggle with consistency in this area because great ball-striking is simply very difficult to achieve.

One way that you can take a 'shortcut' toward hitting better shots is through choking up on the club. By moving your hands up the grip toward the clubhead (or down the grip, depending on how you look at it), you can shorten the effective length of the club, making it easier to hit the ball solidly. When you move your hands closer to the clubhead, your whole swing gets shorter, adding to the control that you have over the club as it moves back and through. If you have trouble finding the sweet spot on a consistent basis, this is one quick adjustment that you could make to instantly find better contact.

As you might suspect, there is a tradeoff for making this change in your swing. When you shorten the club, the gains that you make in control will be lost in distance. Your overall swing speed will be lowered by choking up, meaning that you won't be able to hit the ball as far as you would making the same swing while gripping the club at the end. This is certainly a drawback, but it doesn't necessarily mean that you should ignore choking up as a viable option to improve your game. After all, distance is only useful when you can control it.

If you are spraying the ball all over the course with your current swing, trading a few yards for improved accuracy might be well worth it.

All of the instruction contained below is based on a right-handed golfer. If you happen to play left-handed, please reverse the directions as necessary.

What to Expect When You Choke Up

There are a few things that are going to change in your swing, and in your ball flight, when you choke up on the club. These changes aren't problems necessarily, but you will have to adjust for them properly in order to be satisfied with the ultimate result of your shots. The best way to get used to these changes is through practice, but you can learn about them here first so that you will know what to look for when you get out on the course.

Following is a list of things to expect when you hit shots while choking up on the club.

Shorter distance. This point was covered above, but it bears re-peating. The shots that you hit with a choked-up grip are going to travel shorter than shots with a regular grip, so you need to plan for this change in your club selection. For example, if you would normally hit a seven iron for a standard 150-yard shot, consider using a six when you are planning on choking up. Over time you will learn exactly how much distance you will lose while choking up so you can fine-tune your club selections accordingly.

Lower launch. Most golfers will find that the ball comes out lower when they are choking up on the club. This is mostly to do with the reduced swing speed that you will experience, but it can also be a side effect of making a slightly shorter swing. Whatever the reason, you should be planning on a lower ball flight when choking up on the club. That means that you might not be able to clear a tree that you would have otherwise been able to get over, and it also means that the ball will take a bigger first bounce when it lands. Understanding these differences is important for picking the right club – and planning the right shot – as often as possible.

Pull tendency. While it is easier to hit the ball accurately with a choked-up grip, you might notice that you have a slight tendency to pull the ball to the left with this kind of swing. That mistake is perfectly normal, and many golfers struggle with the same problem. Since your swing is a little bit shorter than usual, your tempo may speed up slightly – which can lead to a pull. Make a conscious effort to slow down your tempo early in the backswing to keep everything on track for a solid strike. If you can maintain a smooth tempo even with your shorter swing, you should be able to start the ball perfectly on your target line.

Potential for higher spin rate on wedges. This is not a rule of thumb that will apply to everyone, but some golfers may find that they impart more backspin on their wedge shots while choking up on the club. Most likely, this is a result of additional hand action through impact. Since you will be holding a thinner part of the grip by moving your hands down, you may end up using your hands more aggressively through the hitting area. When that happens, the clubface can rip under the ball and add a high rate of backspin to the shot. As you are learning how to play using a choked-up grip, watch your spin rates, and adjust your aiming process if you find that you are spinning the ball more with your short clubs.

None of the changes that you will notice from choking up on the club are drastic. Each is a subtle change, but you need to understand them if you are going to adapt your game and make the most of this useful technique. Having the ability to play shots while choking up can help you shoot better scores, but only when you understand all of the small adjustments involved in the process.

How to Choke Up Correctly

The practice is important when learning how to choke up on the club just like it is important when learning any other skill on the course. Many players think that they can just move their hands down a couple of inches and swing away, but there is a little more to it than that. If you wish to play great shots using this technique, the process is going to have to start at the driving range.

You don't really need to do any specialized drills or fancy practice routines in order to learn how to choke up on the club. In fact, if you simply hit some balls while working through the step by step process below, you should quickly become comfortable with this technique.

To start, head to the driving range with your set of golf clubs and a bucket of balls. You can work on hitting choked up shots for the entire practice session, or you can just include working on this shot as part of a longer session. Since you aren't going to be making any major swing changes during this process, you can work on this at any time – even before a round of golf.

For your first shots, use a short club such as a sand wedge or pitching wedge. The short clubs are easier to hit than the long clubs, so starting with a wedge will give you a chance to build some confidence. Once you get the idea of how to hit good shots while choking up, you can then move on to hitting some of your longer clubs.

Place a ball down on the ground in front of you and start to work through your regular pre-shot routine. Prior to taking your stance, everything about this process should be exactly the same as any other shot. Once you have completed your pre-shot routine and selected a target, walk up to the ball and prepare to take your stance.

The process of taking your stance should start with placing the clubhead down behind the ball. With the clubhead resting on the ground behind the ball, put your hands into place on the grip of the club. Depending on how much you wish to choke up, your hands could be anywhere between one inch and several inches below the top of the grip. The formation of your grip shouldn't change – only it's location on the handle of the club.

Once your hands are set on the club, and the club is resting behind the ball, go ahead and take your stance. It is important that you take your stance after you establish your grip, and not before. If you were to plant your feet in the ground prior to creating your grip, you would not be able to accurately position them at the correct distance from the ball. You are going to be standing closer to the ball while choking up than you would be otherwise, so getting your stance right is crucial to your success. Grab the club first, then take your stance, and you will be on track toward making a great swing.

With all of the pre-shot business taken care of, go ahead and hit a few shots. Pay careful attention to your ball flight so you can learn what kind of shots are created when you choke up on the club. Remember to keep great rhythm and balance in your swing – the fundamentals that you have learned for your regular golf swing still apply when choking up on the club.

Hit several wedge shots by going through this step by step process. Once you feel like you have the hang of it, start to hit some longer clubs and test your skills. It will likely take more time to learn how to hit your longer clubs while choking up, but the effort will be worth it in the end. After spending plenty of time working on this process up front, you can then make it a regular part of your practice routine during each visit to the course. Hit at least a few choked up shots during every range visit to keep your skills sharp in this area.

When to Choke Up on the Club

There is a lot to like about choking up on the club. For one thing, it doesn't take very long to learn. After working through the steps above, you could be comfortable hitting choked up shots on the course within the next round or two that you play. Very few skills in golf can be learned and applied that quickly, but since choking up doesn't change very much of your actual swing technique, you can start reaping the benefits almost immediately.

Another great thing about choking up is simply the long list of applications that this method has out on the course. You might be surprised to learn how many different times during an average round that choking up will be a smart choice. In fact, after a short period of time, you will probably be wondering how you ever played golf without knowing how to choke up on the club.

Following is a partial list of the various situations that call for choking up on the club –

Windy conditions. Playing in the wind is always a challenge, but it can be made significantly easier when you have the ability to choke up on your clubs. The changes that choking up makes to your ball flight – specifically lowering the ball flight and taking speed out of the shot – are perfect for dealing with the wind. Contrary to popular belief, you don't want to hit the ball hard when playing in the wind.

Instead, you will be better served to hit soft shots that stay low and take the wind mostly out of play. To hit those low shots that are so great at beating the wind, you will want to choke down on the club at least an inch or two. It is easy to lose your tempo when playing in high winds, so focus on maintaining a nice rhythm while the choked up grip helps you keep the ball under control.

Dangerous approach shots. When hitting an approach shot into a green that is guarded by hazards or deep bunkers, consider choking up to add accuracy to your swing. As long as you aren't an extremely long distance from the green, you should be able to simply take one extra club to reach the target as you choke up on the grip. While you always want to get the ball close to the hole, it is more important on a shot like this to avoid putting yourself in trouble. Choke up to improve your accuracy and find the green safely.

Narrow fairways. You can choke up on your driver and fairway woods just like you can your irons, and the results can be equally as impressive. When you are faced with a narrow tee shot on a par four or par five, think about coming down the grip an inch or two to take a little speed off of the shot and add some control.

Yes, you will sacrifice a few yards of distance, but that trade will be more than worth it if you are able to place the ball right in the center of the fairway. Not every hole needs to be a competition with yourself to see how far you can hit the ball – playing for the position is smart, especially when the fairway isn't giving you much room for error.

Downhill shots. Many amateur golfers, when faced with a downhill shot, like to launch the ball as high into the air as possible so they can watch it soar. This might be fun, but it isn't going to do much for you as far as getting the ball close to the hole is concerned. The fact is that the longer the ball is in the air, the more time it has to drift off line. With that in mind, try hitting your downhill shots using a choked-up grip so you can keep the flight down and limit the hang time. It is always difficult to get a downhill shot perfectly on line, but the task will become a little easier when you choke up on the club.

The four examples above are just some of the opportunities you will have on the course to use your newfound skill of choking up on the club. Don't be afraid to experiment with shots as you make your way through a round – you just might find a great chance to choke up that wasn't mentioned on this list.

Troubleshooting

Compared to some of the other techniques you can try on the golf course, hitting the ball while choking up on the club is pretty simple. However, you may run into some problems along the way, especially at first. If the shots you are hitting with a choked-up grip aren't meeting your expectations, the trouble-shooting points below may be able to help.

Hitting a hook. Even if you don't fight a hook anywhere else on the course, you might find that you hit one from time to time when choking up on the club. This happens because your hands are more active in this kind of swing, so they are able to 'flip' the clubface over and create hook spin. To prevent this from happening, get your lower body more engaged in the downswing. Use your legs and torso to drive the rotation toward the target and your quick hook should be a thing of the past.

Topping the ball. This is a common mistake among golfers who don't have very much experience hitting shots while choking up. Since you are standing slightly closer to the ball at address, you may be tempted to 'stand up' through the shot at impact in order to make room for the club. Of course, you don't need to do that, and the result will often be a topped shot that rolls along the ground. Get rid of this outcome by staying down through the shot and watching the ball until it is struck.

Shank. If you find that you are hitting the occasional shank when choking up on your irons, check to make sure you aren't standing too close to the ball at address. You should move slightly closer to the ball while choking up, but overdoing it can lead to the shanks. Go back to the point about building your stance in order to fix this problem. As long as you set the club-head down first behind the ball prior to placing your feet for the stance, you should be able to position your body correctly.

Choking up on the club is a skill that every golfer should have available. In addition to helping you hit accurate shots and make solid contact, this style of a golf shot is also useful in a wide range of situations. Since this technique just builds upon the other fundamentals already present in your golf swing, it shouldn't take much work to incorporate this shot into your repertoire. Once you see how effective this kind of swing can be, you may find yourself looking for every opportunity to choke up on the club and fire the ball directly at the pin. Choking up won't instantly fix any swing problems that you may have, but it will certainly help you to get the most of your swing, and your game.

CHAPTER 6: TRAJECTORY CONTROL

One of the many things that set tour pros apart from amateurs – even very good ones – is the ability to control the ball's trajectory.

This is an important factor in windy conditions, but also when playing to different pin placements, carrying distant hazards, or hitting a shot that runs after landing.

There's no real magic to altering the height of your shots. It's largely done by changing the ball's position in your stance, which determines the club's effective loft at impact. As a simple rule, the farther up in your stance you play the ball – toward the left foot, for a right-hander – the higher it will fly. Play it farther back, or to the right, to produce a lower flight.

It's important to keep the hands ahead of the ball and the shaft leaning toward the target on iron shots. The farther back you play the ball, the more the shaft will lean.

This "de-lofts" the clubface for a lower trajectory. The same concept applies to chips and bunker shots.

Control Trajectory by Varying Ball Position

The ability to control the trajectory of your shots might seem like a skill that is a bit out of reach. After all, as an amateur golfer, you don't have the control over your ball which is demonstrated by the top pros. However, even if you have a lot of work to do on your game, it is still worth your time to learn how to alter your trajectory on command. Not only will you add some new shots to your game as you learn this skill, but you will also improve the overall quality of your swing in the process.

One of the best ways to control the trajectory of your shots is by varying the ball position you use at the address. When you setup over the ball, you have to determine where you are going to stand in relation to the position of the ball on the ground. Are you going to line up with the ball in the middle of your stance, or up toward your front foot? Or, are you going to play the ball back in your stance, closer to your right foot (for a right-handed golfer)? Choosing your ball position is one of many decisions that need to be made before you can go ahead with a swing. This is an important decision, of course, as it is going to largely determine the type of trajectory you use for the shot.

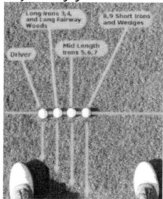

Many amateur golfers make the mistake of trying to make dramatic swing changes when they want to produce a different-than-usual ball flight. Generally speaking, that is just not necessary. Instead of changing your swing in any significant way, try adjusting the location of the ball within your stance. While it is difficult to make swing changes on the fly, it is quick and easy to change where you are standing in relation to the ball. As long as you practice these adjustments before you play – so you know what they will do to the flight of the ball – you can use this method to experience great success.

While it is true that ball position adjustments are a powerful way to change your trajectory, there are some minor swing tweaks which will be needed as well. As mentioned in the previous paragraph, you don't want to make any dramatic or drastic changes to your swing mechanics as you play – but you will need to slightly alter the way you swing the club in order to generate a variety of different ball flights. When you bring together the right ball position with the proper swing technique, impressive results are possible.

All of the content below is based on a right-handed golfer. If you happen to play left-handed, please take a moment to reverse the directions as necessary.

Understanding the Basics

If you are an experienced golfer, you may already understand the basics of how ball position can impact your trajectory. If you are a beginner, you may have no concept of how this works. Either way, it will be beneficial to review the information below. By having a clear understanding of what various ball positions should do to your trajectory, you can quickly dial up the right one needed for the shot at hand.

The following points will outline the basics of how ball position impacts shot trajectory on the golf course.

Move the ball forward to hit higher shots. Moving the ball 'forward' in your stance means moving it closer to your left foot. When you make this adjustment, the club will have more effective loft at impact, and the shot will fly higher than it would when played from farther back in the stance. For example, if you hit a seven iron shot from the middle of your stance, you will likely see an 'average' trajectory in terms of height.

If on your next swing, you move the ball up in your stance by a couple of inches, the next shot should fly higher into the sky (assuming you make solid contact, of course). This minor ball position adjustment is one of the easiest ways to produce higher trajectories on demand. With practice, you will get a feel for how much you need to move your ball position in order to achieve various heights. This equation will change as you hit different clubs from different lies, so there is no substitute for experience when learning what to expect out of your variety of ball position options.

Move the ball back to hit it lower. This was the logical point to follow up on the previous item on the list. If moving the ball forward in your stance is going to help you hit it higher, moving the ball back will obviously help you to hit it lower. It doesn't take much of an adjustment to hit a dramatically lower shot, either.

To continue the previous example, imagine you moved the ball a couple of inches back from the center when hitting your seven iron. While playing from behind center in your stance, you will get an extremely low ball flight capable of cutting through the wind and maybe even offering some bounce and roll after it lands. This is a shot that is useful in many situations around the course, and it is one that every golfer should have in his or her bag.

Stand farther away to hit a draw. When the average golfer speaks of ball position, they are generally talking about moving the ball left or right in their stance, as seen from the address. However, that is only one half of the equation. Also, you need to think about how far you are standing away from the ball. You should have a 'standard' distance you stand from the ball for normal shots, and you can then adjust from there to alter your trajectory. In this case, if you want to hit a draw, you are going to stand a little bit farther away.

Moving back away from the ball will cause your swing to flatten out, and you will be more likely to trace an inside-out path through the hitting area – leading to a draw. Also, with plenty of room between yourself and the ball, you should find it easy to release the club properly at impact. When facing a shot where a draw is absolutely essential, moving back a couple of inches farther away from the ball should do the trick.

Stand closer to the ball to hit a fade. Again, this is another obvious point based on the previous explanation. Standing closer to the ball is going to make it more likely that you will produce a fade based on the adjustments which will take place in your swing. Your swing plane is going to become more upright, meaning you may attack the ball from an outside-in path. Also, it will be hard to release the club fully at impact without as much space between your body and the club, so you will be more likely to hold the face open slightly. When you add it up, you are left with a swing that should produce a reliable left-to-right shot pattern time after time.

The four points above are all you need to know about the basics of controlling your trajectory through the use of a ball position. Wish to hit the ball higher? Move it toward the front of your stance. Need to hit it lower? Move it back a couple of inches. Want to hit a draw or a fade? Stand farther away, or closer, respectively. It will take a little bit of practice to learn how to execute these adjustments, but the basic framework of this part of the game is easy to understand.

Minor Swing Adjustments

As was mentioned in the opening of this chapter, there are a few minor swing adjustments you will need to make in order to optimize your results. These are not dramatic changes, however, they are still quite important. If the ball is going to behave in the manner that you would like while in the air, you need to make a swing which leads it in the correct direction.

Fortunately, there isn't anything you need to do when it comes to favoring a draw or a fade by changing your distance from the ball. If you are trying to curve the ball in one direction or another, you can simply stand closer or farther away and then make your usual swing. The beauty of adjusting your ball position, in this case, is the fact that you don't need to do anything mechanical to alter the direction of the curve. The ball position change does the work for you, so trust it and swing away with confidence.

The same cannot be said for hitting your shots higher or lower. When you move the ball left or right in your stance to change the height of the trajectory, you need to make a couple of associated changes to your technique in order to see good results. Those changes are outlined below.

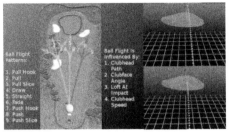

Higher shots. When trying to hit the ball higher, you are going to start by moving the ball slightly to the left in your stance. Once that is done, you can turn your attention to the manner in which you are going to swing the club. The key here is to stay balanced and rotate nicely through the downswing. It will be tempting to slide to the left as you swing down since the ball is going to be resting farther to the left than usual.

This slide to the left would be a mistake. The whole point of adjusting your ball position is to catch the shot just after the bottom of your swing – but if you slide left, you will be shifting the bottom of your swing to the left, negating the benefit of changing your ball position in the first place. Instead of that slide, focus on great rotation while making a full release of the club through impact. It is that release that will allow you to expose all of the lofts of the club to the ball when contact is made.

Lower shots. Most likely, you are going to attempt to hit the ball lower far more often than you will attempt to hit it higher. Of course, you are going to start this process by moving the ball back in your stance. Then, turn your attention to making a controlled, balanced golf swing. Your weight should stay perfectly between your two feet throughout the backswing, and you should keep your head down all the way through impact.

When trying to hit the ball low, you want to restrict your release, so swing only to an abbreviated follow-through to make sure you aren't releasing the club too dramatically. The back of your left wrist should feel firm and flat at impact. It takes some practice to get comfortable with the truncated swing needed to hit low shots, but this will be a powerful weapon in your arsenal once it is mastered.

The best way to learn how to adjust your swing is simply to practice these shots on the range. During your next practice session, spend some time trying to hit shots both higher and lower on command. Through this process, you will learn which adjustments work for your swing, and which ones don't. Once you can reliably produce high and low shots on the driving range, you will be ready to take this newfound skill out onto the course.

Picking Your Spots

It is one thing to learn how to hit a variety of different trajectories – it is another thing to learn how to use those trajectories effectively. Shot selection is an important skill in golf, as hitting the right shots at the right time is almost as important as being able to hit those shots in the first place.

The best comparison in sports that can be made for shot selection in golf is to think about a pitcher in baseball. Any given major league pitcher is going to have at least two different pitches he can throw, and most pitchers will have three or four. In addition to being able to physically throw the pitches, a pitcher also has to pick the right one to throw at the right time. If a pitcher throws a fastball when a curve-ball would have been a better choice, for example, the outcome could be a disaster. Just like the pitcher in baseball, you have to know exactly when to reach for your various trajectories in order to optimize your results.

To get started on improving your shot selection, the first rule of thumb to remember is this – always use your 'stock' shot whenever possible. Your 'stock' shot is the ball flight that will be produced when you make a normal swing with no adjustments. As long as the shot you are facing can be handled with that standard ball flight, you should stick with it and avoid any changes.

You only want to make changes to your game plan when the course forces you to do so.

What kinds of situations could arise which would force you to alter your approach? Consider the following points.

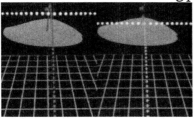

Low shots in the wind. This is probably the most obvious point of all, but it is an important one to remember. When playing in the wind – no matter what direction that wind is blowing – your best bet is to keep the ball low to the ground. Hitting high shots in the wind takes away much of the control you have over the ball, and you never want to give up control in this game. Learning how to hit low shots around a windy golf course will allow you to score much better when conditions are tough.

Low shots to back hole locations. Another great time for a low iron shot is when you are attacking a hole location found in the back of the green. Rather than flying the ball all the way to the hole, and risking a shot that flies over the green, hit a low approach and bounce the ball back toward the cup. There is a greater margin for error with this shot, and you will still have a chance to hit it close in order to setup a birdie putt.

High shots to front hole locations. You aren't going to be able to take the ball in low when hitting an approach to a hole located on the front of the green because you won't have room for the ball to bounce and stop. Therefore, you should hit this shot high and bring it down softly somewhere around the cup.

Aim to the center and curve toward the edges. When facing an approach shot to a green with the hole cut near an edge, try to aim the ball at the center of the putting surface and curve it off of that point. This strategy is ideal because you won't be punished for a straight shot. If the ball flies straight, you will find it in the middle of the green and you can putt it from there. If it does curve in the intended direction, you will have an even better look at your putt.

Use curves to deal with doglegs. When standing on the tee of a par four or par five with a large dogleg in the fairway, use a draw or fade shape as necessary to position your ball in the fairway. Even if you aren't perfectly accurate with these kinds of shots, turning your ball in the same direction as the hole will give you a great chance to wind up with a nice tee shot.

Keep your mind open to various types of shots while on the course, while at the same time always defaulting back to your 'stock' shot whenever possible. Over time, you will develop a style of play which is a nice blend of standard shots and altered ball flights to match the demands of the course.

Ball Position Around the Greens

The trajectory is something you think of when hitting full shots, but it matters in the short game as well. Fortunately, the same general rules apply for chip and pitch shots as they do for full swings, so you can take what you have learned in the long game and apply it to your short game. Need to hit a high chip shot which lands softly on the green? Move the ball up in your stance. Need to pitch the ball low to the ground so it will run out after it lands? Move the ball back closer to your right foot.

When chipping and pitching, you don't need to worry about the curve of the ball, as these shots will not be in the air long enough to draw or fade. However, you still want to pay attention to the distance that you stand from the ball at address. You need to be in a comfortable position, and your arms should have room to swing freely through the hitting area.

As was the case with the full swing, the best thing you can do to find the right ball positions in your short game is to practice. Hit chip and pitch shots from a variety of ball positions to see how the ball reacts both in the air and after it lands. By having as many shots as possible available to you out on the course, you will be able to deal with a wide variety of circumstances that may come up in the short game.

Ball position is a key fundamental in golf. You need to stand in the appropriate position next to the ball in order to create the right type of shot for the situation at hand. Pay close attention to this part of your game during upcoming practice sessions and you should find that it can quickly help you to play better golf on the course. Good luck!

CHAPTER 7: BALL POSITION

I f your stance, posture, and club length are all correct, but your ball-striking is weak, the solution could be as checking your golf ball position. Here's a primer:

If your ball position is too far forward in your stance (toward the foot closest to the target, left for a right-hander), the club will be released too early. Your shots will fly too low because the clubface is closed at impact.

If the ball is too far back in your stance, the club will not have enough time to release, causing high, pushed shots to the right due to an open clubface.

If you stand too far from the golf ball, you'll hit weak, right-veering shots off the club's toe.

If you stand too close, you may shank or pull the ball.

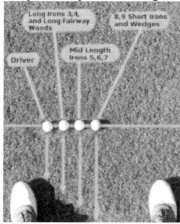

Let"s look at how ball position should vary based on the club type (playing from a flat lie):

Short irons (wedges, 9-iron and 8-iron) should be played with a ball position in the center portion of your stance. Because of their upright lie angles, you should always hit the ball first, then the ground, producing a fairly deep divot.

Middle irons (5 through 7) should be played with the ball slightly forward of center (about 1-2 ball widths). This means the ball will be slightly closer to the foot which is closest to the target. These clubs have a somewhat flatter lie angle than the short irons, so your divot should be slightly shallower.

Long irons (2-4) and fairway woods should be played with the ball about 2-3 ball widths forward of center. Your swing will have more of a sweeping action, with the ball struck directly at the bottom of the swing arc and little or no divot.

Driver shots should be played farthest forward (even with the left heel) in order to strike the ball on the upswing.

Once you understand proper ball position basics for each club type, you can personally fine-tune your positioning. Swing each club and mark where it hits the ground in relation to your stance. Then place the ball at the beginning (back) edge of the mark. Your ball-striking will improve and you'll hit fewer fat shots (club hitting the ground first) and thin shots (bottom edge of the club hitting the middle or top of the ball).

Dialing in the Perfect
Golf Ball Position

There are a number of important fundamentals related to the golf swing, and proper ball position is certainly on that list. Correct golf ball placement at address is vital to the consistency of your performance on the course because you can only control your ball flight if you are putting the ball at the same point in your stance shot after shot. Many golfers struggle with an inconsistent golf ball position, which puts them in an uphill battle to hitting good shots. You might think there is a problem with your golf swing itself because of the poor shots you are hitting, but the trouble could be hiding in your golf ball placement all along.

The problem for most golfers is that golf ball position, and golf setup position in general, just doesn't seem that important. Most golfers focus the vast majority of their practice time on the swing itself, from the time the club starts moving back until the moment it strikes the ball. However, much of the quality of your swing has to do with what happens prior to ever starting the club in motion. If you are able to put yourself in a great position at address – and put the ball in the right position as well based on the club you are using – making a good swing instantly gets much easier. Most golf teachers can tell how good a player is just by watching them setup to the ball because it reveals so much about the swing that is about to happen.

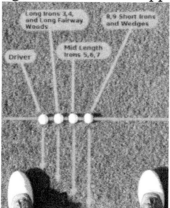

Among the common ball position mistakes that golfers make is thinking that they can use the same golf ball position for different clubs. For the majority of players, that just isn't going to work. When you learn how to adjust your golf ball position for different clubs, you will give each of those clubs the chance to perform at their best.

Since all of your clubs are slightly different in terms of lie angle, loft, and length, it only makes sense that your ball position would vary as you move through your bag. It might seem like a lot of work to develop your own golf ball position chart for each club, but the effort will be worth it in the end. Knowing where you want to position the ball with each club, and then doing it time after time accurately, is something that can separate a good golfer from an average one.

When talking about golf ball placement in your stance, there are really two categories to deal with – woods and irons. Since the swing you use, and the kind of impact you make, with your woods and your irons, is different, there are different rules that apply to the ball positioning you will look for. Try to keep the two separate in your mind and remember that what applies to ball position for irons isn't necessarily going to be true with your woods.

It is important to note before we get started with the instruction on ball position that all of the directions below are based on a right-handed golfer. For those of you who play left-handed, please reverse the instructions to make sure they apply correctly to your game.

The Basic Idea

Just like anything else you do on the golf course, it is important to understand why you need to place the ball in the right position shot after shot. Only when you are clear on that point will you be likely to take the time and effort it requires to execute proper ball position all throughout a round.

It's not breaking news that one of the main goals in your golf swing is to make solid contact with the ball at impact. With a driver, that means finding the sweet spot while the ball is sitting up on a tee. With your irons, that means hitting the ball with a downward impact just slightly before your club hits the ground and takes a divot. Without making solid contact at impact, you will have a hard time hitting the ball the right distance, and you will hit plenty of off-line shots as well.

So we know that making good contact is essential – but what role does ball position play in that process? Think about it this way. Imagine that you were playing basketball, and you were standing at the line shooting free throws. Which of the following would be easier – shooting free throws at a stationary basket, or one that was moving from side to side? Obviously, it would be easier to shoot free throws at a stationary basket. No matter what sport you are talking about, hitting a moving object is almost always going to be harder.

Inconsistent ball position is essentially a moving target for your golf swing to hit. If you stand over your shot on the second hole and the ball is in a different position than it was on the first hole, your swing is going to have to adjust. Could you make the adjustment and still hit a good shot? Sure, maybe. But you shouldn't have to. Getting the ball in the right position on every single shot-makes the work that your golf swing has to do that much easier.

Not having to swing at a 'moving' target is one great reason to work on your ball position. But there are others. For instance, if you hope to develop your game to the point where you can create different ball flights for different situations on the course, you will need to know how your ball position influences that skill. Placing the ball back in your stance farther will generate a lower ball flight while moving it up an inch or two should help you get the ball higher in the air. Also, depending on the specific mechanics of your swing, moving the ball up or back can (or in or out) can also change whether you hit a draw or a fade.

To review, a good ball position makes it easier for your swing to repeat correctly shot after shot, hole after hole. It allows you to hit a bigger variety of shots and hit them with more consistency. Golf is a game where consistency is hard to find, so getting more of it in any way you can is always a good thing.

Ball Position for Woods

In this section, we are mostly going to be focused on getting the ball position right for your driver, but the basic idea remains the same for your three wood, five wood, etc. Because of the design of your driver, with a flatter lie angle than your irons, you want to swing it in a way that promotes a 'flat' impact with the ball. That means that instead of the clubhead moving downward through impact like it should be doing with your irons, the driver should contact the ball when it is moving roughly parallel with the ground. If anything, you actually want the driver head to be moving slightly back up away from the ground at impact, as that will give you the best chance at an optimal launch angle and carry distance.

To find the right ball position for your driver, head to the practice tee with your driver and plenty of balls to hit. You will also need an extra club that you can lay along the ground as an alignment aid. Place a golf ball on a tee, and then set your alignment club on the ground such that the grip of the club is pointed directly at the ball, forming a 90* angle with your target line. Now, take your golf setup position with that alignment club lying on the ground between your feet. To start with, the club should be just barely touching your left heel – that will mean that the ball is lined up with the inside of your left foot – perfect for most golfers when hitting a driver.

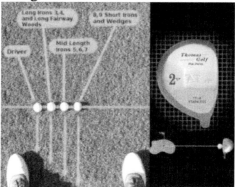

Try hitting a few shots from this traditional ball position and check the results. If the ball flight looks exactly like you want it, you are finished! This will be a successful ball position for plenty of golfers, so you might find that you don't need to do anything else to optimize the ball position of your driver. However, some players may need to make a few more adjustments to find just the right spot.

If you notice that you are hitting most of the drives low on the clubface in this position, that likely means that the club is moving back up too much at impact, and you need to move the ball back in your stance slightly. It is important to understand that a small change can lead to a big difference in results, so try moving the ball back in your stance only a little bit at a time until you find a good spot for your swing. Throughout the process, use your alignment club as a guide to making sure the ball is actually in the position that you think it is.

On the other side of the equation, you might need to move the ball up in your stance a little farther if you are hitting most of your tee shots too high on the clubface. This is an indication that the clubhead is moving too much down through impact, and your drives are probably floating high into the air and falling down relatively short. Slide the ball forward an inch or so at a time until you are able to hit the sweet spot of your driver swing after swing.

The great thing about working on your driver ball position is that the ground should be flat under your feet for every tee shot, meaning you won't need to make any other adjustments to your ball position out on the course. Once you settle on the right spot for you and your swing, you can probably leave it alone and just work on becoming as consistent and repeatable as possible. As you will see in the next section, things are not so simple when it comes to your irons.

Ball Position for Irons

The ball position that you use for your irons is always going to be more important than it is with your driver. Make no mistake – it is still important with the driver – but it is absolutely essential when hitting iron shots off of the turf. If you are unable to find a good ball position for your irons, and then repeat it shot after shot, you are going to have very little chance of playing good golf on a consistent basis.

The proper ball position for an iron shot is right at the bottom of your swing arc, which should match up with your center of gravity at the point of impact. While that might sound pretty simple, actually getting the ball in that spot time after time is pretty complicated. The problem is that as your swing gets longer with your longer irons, the way your body works and moves in the swing will change. Therefore, you can't use the same ball position for all of your irons and expect to get great results.

To get started working out a golf ball position chart for your irons, you should head to the practice range and start with the shortest club in your bag, other than the putter. For most golfers, this will be either a sand wedge or a lob wedge. Use the same trick with an alignment club from above and get the ball positioned perfectly in the middle of your stance – halfway between your right and left foot at address. This is going to be your 'baseline' ball position. Hit a few shots with the ball centered in your stance and see how it feels. Hopefully, this will be about right for you when hitting your shortest wedge.

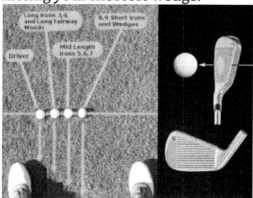

Why start at the center of your stance? Because, we are hoping to catch the ball position to the bottom of your swing, which should be right in the middle of your stance for a wedge. When hitting a short shot, you don't want to have any noticeable lateral movement in your swing – it should all be rotational. So, the center of gravity that you have at the start of the swing should be approximately the same as it is at impact. Therefore, the middle of your stance should be the perfect ball position for your wedge shots.

As you move up through your set of irons, the ball should gradually move forward in your stance, a little bit at a time. With each club, this change in ball position should only be an inch or so, at the most. You will need to take time and care to find just the right spot in your stance and use your alignment club to help you achieve this properly. Hit a few balls with each of your irons to make sure that the ball position you are using is going to produce a ball flight that you are happy with.

Your iron ball position should be a sliding scale that gradually moves from the center of your swing up toward the inside of your front foot. The longest iron in your bag should be the one that uses a ball position that is closest to your front foot. So, if your three iron is the longest iron you have, that ball position should be the farthest left as you look down from the address. The progression in ball position from wedge to long iron should be smooth and gradual so that it can match the center of gravity in your swing at impact correctly.

Finding the perfect ball position with your irons is going to take some experimentation and some practice. At first, you are going to have to really think about each club and where the ball should be placed – but it should become more natural over time. In the final section, we will discuss how you can make the process of finding the right ball position easier to happens on the course without much thinking.

How to Make it Repeatable

It is one thing to be able to find a good ball position on the driving range and hit some quality shots during your practice sessions – but it is something else to do it on the course. When playing for real, you won't be able to put an alignment club down on the ground to help you, and you won't get multiple chances to get it right. You have to get your ball position right the first time, every time if you are going to play your best.

In order to take what you have learned on the driving range with you out onto the course, you are going to need to have a pre-shot routine in place that helps you find your ball position. The following step-by-step system is one that many golfers use, and it is one of the easiest ways to make sure you are taking your stance in the right position.

To start, stand behind your ball with the club you are going to use in hand. Look down the hole toward your target, and picture hitting a good shot. Try to be as detailed as you can be with your visualization, including the ball flight you want to use and where you want the ball to land.

With that done, walk up to your ball and get ready to take your stance. Before placing your feet in position, set the club down carefully behind the ball. Let the club rest naturally on the ground, so that the sole of the club is flat on the turf. You will use the position of the club to build the rest of your stance.

Next, place your left foot in position relative to the ball and your club so that you can grab onto the grip of the club comfortably. This is where your ball position will be determined. So, if you are hitting a driver, you will want to place your left foot such that the ball is lined up with the inside of your heel (or whatever point is right for your swing). At this point, your right foot should still be set back from your stance and not locked into place.

Once you are happy with the position of your left foot and your hands are on the club, you can bring your right foot up and complete the stance. Since you are already in position with the club and your left foot, the only thing you need to do with the right foot is set it down wherever is comfortable for your stance. Just like that, you have completed a stance and the ball should be in a good position.

While the instructions above might sound like a long and complicated process, it will get easier and faster with a little practice. In fact, you should try working through this routine before every shot you hit on the driving range as a way of ingraining it into your process. Even after just a few driving range sessions of working on this technique, you will find that your pre-shot routine is quickly a natural part of your game.

Proper golf ball placement in your stance is one of the fundamentals of the game that you just can't afford to ignore. Spending time working on the moving parts of your golf swing is great, but it can all be wasted if you don't get setup properly, to begin with. Work on making your pre-shot routine and address the position as consistent as possible, and you will likely find that your actual swing doesn't need as much work as you thought it did. Golf ball position might not be the most exciting thing to practice, but you will put in the time if you are serious about finding lower scores out on the course.

CHAPTER 8: GRIP PRESSURE

An important but oft-overlooked factor in producing maximum distance is correct golf club grip pressure. Here's why it's so crucial:

If you grip the club too tightly, your muscles become firm and rigid with less flexibility. This will reduce your swing speed, and the clubhead won't release at the correct time through the impact zone.

Alternatively, a grip that is too loose reduces the control of the club and decreases your ability to hit the sweet spot consistently.

The right amount of grip pressure is difficult to convey in words, but getting it right could add five to 20 yards to your drives. Try this:

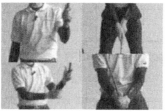

To get the feel for the right amount of grip pressure, hold a club in front of you pointing vertically to the sky. Your sand wedge works well for this as it typically has the heaviest head.

For a right-handed player, put your left-hand on the bottom of the grip with just enough pressure in your last three fingers to keep the club from falling or leaning over from its vertical position.

Add the right-hand so that it is in the correct grip position. This hand should have essentially no pressure, yet still, make full contact with the grip and work in concert with the left-hand.

Once you have this correct golf club grip, you will feel a bit of controlling pressure in the last three fingers of your left-hand, with a very small amount of pressure in the two middle fingers of your right-hand. Try to maintain this pressure throughout your swing. Once you get the hang of this, you will achieve your maximum swing speed and distance, without losing accuracy.

Dialing in the Perfect Grip Pressure in Golf

It is tempting when working on the golf swing to only pay attention to the major points. Things like swing plane and shoulder turn occupy the minds of most golfers, and for good reason – they are key elements to creating the kind of ball flight that you are looking for. However, there are countless other details contained within the swing that can have just as big of an impact on the outcome of your shots. Only when you are able to handle all of these various details correctly are you going to be able to play up to your potential.

Grip pressure in golf is one of those small details that is often overlooked. Even if you know that a light grip pressure in golf is ideal, you might not have spent too much time thinking about it or working on it during your practice sessions. It is easy to let your mind get caught up in other areas of the swing while forgetting that the pressure you put on the grip with your hands has a lot to do with where the ball is going to end up. From tee to green, grip pressure in golf is a major factor that serious golfers will spend time working on in order to make big improvements.

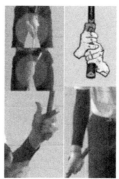

One of the challenges in learning how to hold a golf club without pressure is that you can't see the grip pressure that other players are using. For example, many golfers look to the pros on Tour to learn their techniques and try to copy their swings as closely as possible. While that might work okay for copying static positions such as the top of the backswing, you can't actually see how tightly they are holding the club. Learning to take the proper light grip pressure in golf is something that you have to develop on your own through practice and attention to detail.

The importance of this fundamental extends all the way down to even the shortest shots on the course. In fact, having a light grip pressure on the putting green might be even more important than when you are hitting a full shot. Think about it this way – the tighter you hold the club, the less feel you are going to have in your hands during the shot. You want to make sure you have plenty of feel on your short game shots, so a light grip pressure is essential. While your grip will naturally get a little tighter as the clubs get longer and the swings get harder, keeping your hands and forearms as relaxed as possible will benefit you greatly.

The instructions included below are written for a right-handed golfer. left-handed players will simply need to reverse the directions so that they are applied correctly.

How Light Should You Go?

Obviously, there is a point along the grip pressure spectrum where you would be holding the club too lightly. You need to maintain control of the swing throughout the swing, and you definitely don't want it flying out of your hands on the follow-through. Therefore, the challenge in terms of learning how to hold a golf club without pressure is striking the perfect balance between too tight and too light. The only way to get there is by experimenting on the practicing range.

When you are hitting practice balls on the driving range, you have the opportunity to tweak different parts of your swing and check out the results. Experimenting with different grip pressures is the best way to find the right amount of pressure to optimize your swing. While all golfers should benefit from a light grip, the exact amount of pressure that will work best is going to vary some from player to player.

To get started, use one of your wedges and hit a few short shots on the range. You don't want to be hitting long shots just yet because it is easier to experiment while hitting pitches of only 40 or 50 yards. Hit five shots toward a target about 50 yards away using your normal grip pressure. Next, hit five more shots with a slightly lighter grip pressure and see how they feel. Do you still have complete control of the club throughout the shot? If so, do another set of five while making your grip even a little more relaxed. Continue this process until you reach a point where the club starts to feel too unstable in your hands.

The grip pressure you want to use in your swing is the lightest one that still feels stable and in control. Don't judge it so much by the results of the shots you are hitting, as those will improve with practice – instead, focus on the feeling that you get in your hands when swinging the club. The club should feel light and free to move quickly through the hitting area. With just a little bit of practice, you will start to wonder how you ever played with just a tight grip previously.

Now that you have found a comfortable grip pressure for your pitch shots, gradually increase the distance that you are hitting the ball on the range. Move up to a full swing with that same wedge, then reach for longer and longer clubs until you arrive at the driver. As mentioned before, it might be necessary to squeeze a little tighter as the clubs get longer, but not too much. Even with the driver, you want the grip to feel comfortable and relaxed so the club is free to move through the hitting area as quickly as possible.

It should be noted that the quality of your grips on the golf clubs that you use is important toward helping you maintain a light grip pressure. If your grips are worn or slippery you will need to hang on tighter just to control the club. Try to keep your grips as clean as possible, and replace them periodically before they get too worn down. Also, if you use a golf glove, make sure it is in good condition and dry so it forms a secure connection with the club.

Adjustments to Your Swing

While making swings using a lighter grip pressure has the potential to do great things for your game, it can also cause some problems at first. If you have been playing with a tighter grip up until this point, you will probably experience some challenges as you try to transition into a more relaxed grip. However, after a few minor adjustments to your technique and some time spent practicing, you should be able to get on track and start hitting great shots.

The following are three basic adjustments that you may need to make to your swing in order to accommodate your new, lighter grip pressure. All of these points may not apply to you, so work on them on the range to see what helps you swing better, and what does not.

More aggressive lower body rotation. Using a lighter grip pressure means that your hands are going to have less influence over the movement of the club – especially in the downswing. This is a good thing for the most part, but it can change the dynamics of your current swing. Up until now, you may have been trying to get the clubface square at impact by using your hands to force the release of the club through impact.

That isn't going to work as well with a lighter grip, so that job is going to be transferred to your lower body. Use your legs and hips to rotate your whole body toward the target and allow the club to come along for the ride. This type of swing will help you build more speed in your swing while also improving your timing. Keep your hands out of the action as much as possible and let the rotation of your body swing the club.

Maintain a good tempo. If you are squeezing the club tightly throughout the shot, you can sometimes get away with an uneven tempo because you are just forcing the club to go where you need it with your hands. This isn't a great way to swing the club, but it is what many amateur players do. Getting away from this habit is a step in the right direction, however, you will need to focus on maintaining good tempo throughout your swing if you are going to make it work. Any kind of a rushed motion will throw off the sequencing of the shot, leading to all sorts of problems. Focus on tempo and allow your swing to build speed gradually as the club follows the turning of your body.

Hit down through the shot. Like many amateur players, there is a good chance you currently use too much of your right-hand to 'scoop' the ball up into the air rather than hitting down through it at impact. If that is the case, then switch to a lighter grip pressure is going to cause you some challenges at first. You need to trust the club to do the work of getting the ball into the air for you. Hit down through the shot with your irons, take a divot, and watch the ball climb into the air and hopefully head straight for the target.

All of the mechanics of your swing are interconnected, so changing one can have a trickle-down effect on many others. That isn't necessarily a bad thing, but it is something to be aware of as you make an effort to lighten your grip pressure. Don't expect to just take a lighter grip onto the course and start hitting great shots all day long. Once you successfully adjust your grip, you will then need to alter your swing slightly to facilitate the grip change. Only when all of those tweaks come together just right will you start to enjoy the fruits of your labor.

On the Greens

Using proper grip pressure when putting is every bit as important as when you are swinging the club for a full shot, if not more so. Feel is the name of the game on the putting green, and you want as much feedback coming up the putter and into your hands as possible. Light grip pressure should be easier to achieve in this setting, as well, considering the fact that you only have to rock the putter back and forth rather than swing it around your body.

One of the main benefits of using a lighter grip on the putting green is improved speed control. Most golfers focus on getting the line of their putts right, but speed control is even more important because it allows you to leave the ball close to the hole for an easy second putt. By letting the putter hang from your hands in a relaxed manner gives you the best chance to swing it back and forth freely and roll the ball nicely up next to the cup. Squeezing tightly onto the grip of the putter will only serve to reduce the feel you have in your hands for the shot, making it far more difficult to get the distance correct. While professional golfers have all kinds of different putting techniques that they use to get the ball into the hole, one thing they all share in an effort to keep the grip as light as they can.

To work on your own putting grip pressure, start by hitting one-handed putts from close range. First, hit these putts with only your left-hand, and then switch to hitting some with only your right-hand. Doing this will help you feel how the putter should be swinging through the ball, rather than being forced through by your arms and hands. You won't have as much control with only one hand on the grip, so your only option will be to let it swing freely. After rolling a few short putts with each hand from a close distance, put both hands back on the putter and focus on rolling the ball with light grip pressure. Hopefully, the one-handed drills will have helped you get this feeling just right.

Another element to putter grip pressure that is often overlooked is the pressure that you can feel when putting. If you get nervous before a certain putt, your body may naturally grip the putter tighter as a response to the pressure that you are feeling at that moment. Even if this only happens from time to time on the course, it can come up when you are facing a big putt and cause you to perform below your ability level. Having the capability to control your nerves and maintain a light grip under pressure is something that the best putters are able to do. Following are a few tips to help you work on that skill –

Take a deep breath. There is nothing like a long, deep breath to relax your muscles and clear your mind. If you can feel yourself getting nervous on the putting green, take a step back, close your eyes briefly, and take a long breath in and out. This simple trick can go a long way toward slowing down your tempo, relaxing your mind, and softening your grip on the club.

Focus on the read. It is important that you center your mind on properly reading the line in front of you – not what might be on the line if you make or miss the putt. Get your mind locked in on the details of the putt such as how much it is going to break left or right, and how much up or downhill it might be. By immersing yourself in the process of the read, you can actually 'forget' about what is at stake.

Let your mind wander. This tip is basically the opposite of the previous one, but it can be beneficial as well. If you have an extra moment on the green while waiting for your playing partners to putt, look off into the distance and let your mind wander onto something other than golf. It doesn't matter what it is, as long as it isn't golf-related. After a few moments, bring yourself back to the task at hand and refocus on the putt you are facing. This mental 'break' should help relax you and relieve some of the pressure that has been building.

Maintaining a light grip pressure is a technique that you can practice, but it also has to do with managing your nerves and your emotions. Using the tips above can help you to keep your mind in a good place and make sure that your grip doesn't get too tight when the pressure is on. Now that you know how to hold a putter without pressure, get out onto the practice green and start working on your new stroke.

Around the Greens

Putts aren't the only short shots that you need to be concerned about. Playing shots from around the green with a soft touch requires the same kind of light grip pressure that you have been working on in your swing and with your putter. The lessons you have learned regarding how to hold a putter without pressure are similar to those you need to learn when playing chip shots and pitches from around the green. A tight grip is never a good thing when trying to hit a delicate shot, so relax your grip and your chipping should quickly improve.

Much like your putting practice from above, try hitting some short chip shots with only one hand on the club at a time. This is going to be much more difficult than it was with your putter, but you are trying to accomplish the same goal. The weight of the clubhead on your wedge should swing the club back and through with minimal effort from you. Once you can successfully get the ball into the air with both your right and left-handed chips, use both hands once again and hit a few more. Of course, you are to remain focused on light grip pressure and you want to feel the weight of the club dropping onto the back of the ball.

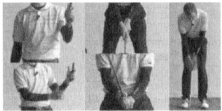

Proper setup technique at address will make it easier to chip the ball with soft hands through impact. Make sure that your weight is leaning left toward the target when you get ready to hit a chip. By leaning a little left, you will be setting up the downward angle of attack that is critical for hitting solid chips shots. Since your grip pressure is going to be light, you can rely on your hands to route the club down into the ball. Lean left to set your shoulders on a downhill slant, then just rock the club back and through to chip the ball cleanly out of the grass.

Chipping is an area of the game that many amateurs struggle with more than any other – and using a lighter grip can help to solve that struggle. When you squeeze too tight before a chip shot, you put pressure in your hands and forearms that work to prevent a smooth swing of the club. Without that smooth rhythm, the club is usually forced down at the ball with all kinds of bad results occurring from there. Give the lighter grip pressure a try and you will be amazed at how much your short game can be transformed.

Any time you alter your grip on the golf course, you can expect there to be some growing pains along the way. Make sure to put in plenty of practice time with your new, lighter grip, and be prepared to make a few other adjustments to your technique to bring everything together. There may be some work required, but it will be more than worth it when you see the results start to take shape out on the course.

CHAPTER 9: AIMING CLUBHEAD

The correct alignment of the golf club is very important. If the clubhead is in the correct position at address, it will ensure the clubface is in line with the shots intended target line. Otherwise, you'll be prone to offline shots.

A clubhead that's misaligned by just a few degrees can send the ball many yards off-target. Additionally, your mind's eye will influence you to swing off plane, causing shots to stray even farther.

Here's how to align a golf club for accurate shots:

Putters: Most golfers find putters easiest to aim, as most have built-in alignment aids. To line up properly, stand behind the ball, pick out your target line, then address the ball aiming your putter's alignment feature along this line.

Drivers, hybrids, and fairway woods: Some woods and hybrids have a marking on the crown of the clubhead. Depending on the shape and levelness of this marking, it can be used when setting up the club to point down your target line. (A marking that is a straight line and level to the ground is the most helpful and accurate, while a mark or line on a curved surface can be misleading.)

Just like the putter, with these clubs, you should first stand behind the ball and pick out your target line. it's very helpful to find an intermediate target near the ball and in line with the target. Then, using the sighting aid on the crown of the clubhead, you can accurately aim the clubhead at the intermediate target. Without such aid, you'll have to trust your eyes to align the face properly.

Irons: Irons can be the most difficult to aim for. Since the toe is higher than the heel, the top edge (and club's shape) will appear to be angled many degrees in the open position. This has a significant effect on your mind and adds extra difficulty when using irons. Like all the other club types, a straight-line indicator that is level to the ground is the most helpful for accurately lining up to your target line. (Thomas Golf brand makes the only irons available with this patented feature.) Follow the same procedure as with your woods or hybrids; pick an intermediate target near the ball and aim the clubface at this spot.

The Overlooked Skill of Aiming in Golf

At its very core, golf is a target-based game. You might not think of golf in the same way that you would, say, archery, but the ideas are actually very similar. You pick out a specific target, then attempt to get an object as close to that target as possible. If you are able to get close to the target on a consistent basis, you will be successful. Despite the similarities, most people would pay far more attention to getting their bow and arrow lined up perfectly with the bulls-eye on an archery target than they would make sure their golf club is aimed precisely at the target. Instead, most golfers simply place the club behind the ball, take one or two quick looks at the hole, and then swing away.

Obviously, this is a mistake. Aiming your club – and the rest of your body – properly is one of the most important skills you can have on the golf course. It doesn't do you any good to hit straight shots if your club isn't aimed at the target in the first place. In that case, all you would end up with is a shot that flies in a straight line to a destination that you didn't want to reach. Only when you can combine quality ball-striking with proper aim will you be able to hit good shots hole after hole.

If you are a golfer who is serious about improving your game, the aim is something that you should put high on your priority list. Just like any other part of your swing, aiming correctly at the target takes practice and a consistent routine. Work on your aiming ability on the driving range prior to every shot that you hit and your ability to aim accurately on the course should improve dramatically.

The good news is that aiming your club directly at the target is actually one of the easier parts of playing good golf – as long as you have a plan and know what you are trying to do. In addition to helping you get the ball close to the hole, aiming properly can give you a boost of confidence as well. When you are sure that your club is aimed perfectly at the target that you have selected, you can relax your mind and focus on the task of making a good swing. Without that confidence, you might find that your mind never really focuses on swing mechanics because it is still worried about the accuracy of your aim. Get the aim right, quiet your mind, and great swings can follow.

All of the instructions contained below are written for a right-handed golfer. If you are a left-handed player, simply reverse the directions as needed to make sure they apply properly to your game.

The Difference Between the Target Line and the Target

There is an important piece of the puzzle that many amateur golfers get wrong, so it is important to clear it up before we get too far into the discussion of improving your aim. The difference between the target line and target in golf is subtle, but crucial in learning how to aim a golf shot properly. Getting your aim right depends entirely on understanding what each of these terms means, and how they apply to your shots.

Target. This is where you want your ball to end up when all is said and done. As you get ready to hit a shot, you should be evaluating all of the factors that are going to affect that shot – distance, elevation change, wind, hazards, etc. – prior to selecting a final target. It is important to note that your target does not have to be the hole itself.

For example, if you are playing an approach shot into a green that is guarded by a water hazard, and the hole is cut close to that water, you may choose to pick a target that is safely on the other side of the green. This shot might not get close to the hole, but it should avoid the pond and save you a penalty shot. Each and every single shot that you hit on the golf course should have a target.

Target line. This is the line that you intend to start your shot on. It is not, however, always going to be a straight line right toward your target. Most golfers hit shots with some degree of fade or draw in the air, meaning the target line needs to account for that curve in order to get the ball successfully to the target in the end.

So, if you are hitting a 6-iron into the green and have decided to pick the hole itself as your target, you might actually need to aim right or left of the hole to account for your ball flight. Very few, if any, golfers can actually hit the ball in a straight line with any amount of consistency. Therefore, understanding how to adjust your target line to take your ball to the target is really the key skill in aiming your shots.

Knowing how to aim a golf shot properly comes down to understanding the relationship between the target and target line. Once you have picked out a target, you will then think about your intended ball flight and decide on an appropriate target line. Countless golfers make the mistake of simply aiming right at their target on every shot, and the results are predictably disappointing.

A Simple Formula for Getting It Right

There are two inherent problems when trying to aim your golf club correctly. The first is that the target can be hundreds of yards away, while the ball is lying at your feet. It is difficult to aim accurately at something that is so far away from where you are standing. The other problem is that you are standing next to your target line at the address, not on top of it.

Going back to the archery example from earlier, you would be able to look right down the target line while getting ready to take the shot. That is not the case in golf. Therefore, you are going to need to develop a system for aiming the club that takes away these problems and gives you the best chance to aim the clubface directly down your target line.

Following is a step-by-step process meant to help you fine-tune your ability to aim the clubface. If you work on following this routine consistently on the driving range, it should become second nature when you head out onto the course.

Pick your target. The first step should always be to select the target you are going to have for the shot at hand. As mentioned above, that doesn't necessarily have to be the hole itself. On a tee shot, you will need to pick a spot in the fairway where you wish to have the ball end up. On an approach, you might aim directly at the flag or you might aim for a safer part of the green away from potential trouble. No matter where you are intending to have the ball finish, this should always be the first step of your process.

Pick your club. Only select the club you are going to use for a given shot after you have decided on the target. Too many golfers do this part in reverse – they grab a club first, then pick a target based on what club they are holding. That is backward and can lead to poor results. Always select your target prior to picking out a club. Once the target is selected, choose the club you are most confident can handle the shot successfully.

Pick your target line. What kind of shape is this shot going to have? Will it be a draw or a fade? Most likely, you will have one kind of shot that you will hit the vast majority of the time around the course. So, if you are a player who generally fades the ball from left to right, you should plan on that kind of ball flight for the majority of your shots. When picking out a target line, picture the path of the ball through the air and work backward until you find a line that will allow you to hit the shot you are envisioning.

Pick an intermediate target. This is the most important step of the whole process and one that most amateur players skip over. While standing behind your ball looking down the target line, find a spot just a foot or two in front of your ball that is directly on your chosen target line. It could be a blade of grass that is taller than the others, a small leaf, a piece of dirt – anything. As you start to look on the ground in front of your ball, you will be surprised at just how many different options you have for your intermediate target. Once you find that short-range target, lock your eyes onto it and walk up to take your stance.

Set the club. As you build your stance, start by setting the club-head down behind the ball and aim it perfectly at your inter-mediate target. Since you have chosen a short-range target that is only a couple of feet in front of your ball, the task of getting aligned correctly should be simple. You don't even need to look down the fairway toward your eventual target if you don't want to – as long as you are lined up with the short-range target, you can be sure you are aligned properly for the real target as well.

That's it. Those five steps should take you from start to finish through the process of getting your clubface aimed perfectly down the target line. It might sound like a lot of work right now, but after some practice, you will get to a point where you can do all five steps in just a matter of seconds. On the driving range, practice going through this routine while hitting short pitch shots of only 30 or 40 yards. This exercise will help you evaluate how accurately you are aiming, and if you tend to error to the right or left. Over time, you should notice that your aim continues to improve and you will start to hit more shots right at your target.

Setting Your Body Position to Match

Now that you know how to aim your clubhead, it is important that you know how to aim your body as well. While the clubhead is the key piece of the puzzle that absolutely must be aimed down the target line, it will make your job far easier if your body is properly aligned as well. The goal is to set your shoulders, knees, and feet parallel with the target line so that everything is pointing in the same direction. Many amateur players struggle with at least one of these elements falling out of place – which means there has to be compensation somewhere during the swing in order to get back on track.

First, we will focus on the job of getting your feet lined up parallel to the target. This is the best place to start because when your feet are lined up correctly, it becomes pretty easy to get your knees and shoulders to follow along. If you followed the step-by-step directions above for getting your aim right, you should already know that you need to set the clubhead down behind the ball first before setting your feet.

This is critical. Once the clubhead is down behind the ball and aimed properly, you can then use the position of the clubface to guide your stance. Step into place first with your right foot, then with your left. Try to visualize two lines on the ground below you – one that is your target line, and one that is a line running across the toes of both of your feet. Are these lines parallel? If so, you have done a good job taking your stance.

Of course, it might not be easy at first to accurately picture these lines. Therefore, it can be helpful to use a visual aid on the driving range to reinforce these lessons. Before hitting a shot, take two extra clubs out of your bag and lay them down on the ground. One of these clubs should be set along the target line, while the other is set along your toe line.

Stand behind them to make sure they are parallel, then step into the shot. Now when you look down, you can use the shafts of these extra clubs to make completely sure that you are lined up properly. Knowing how to aim your body in the golf swing comes down to getting these lines correct.

With your feet sorted out, the rest of your body may already be in a proper position from which to swing. As long as you have a good athletic posture at address, your shoulders and knees are most likely going to fall right into place stacked above your feet. However, you might want to get some video evidence of this just to be sure.

Ask a friend to take a quick video of your stance from behind so you can see how everything is lining up. Ideally, the lines formed by your feet, knees, and shoulders should all match, and all be running parallel to the left of the actual target line. Even if you think you are aiming correctly, taking videos can provide a nice confirmation that you are on track.

The Strategic Side of Aiming in Golf

All of the golf aiming tips offered to this point have been technical in nature, regarding the physical task of learning how to aim your clubhead. However, there is a mental side to the equation of aiming as well that might be just as important. Specifically, picking good targets for your shots is a skill that you need to develop as you continue through your journey as a golfer.

Selecting targets properly in golf is a combination of good strategy and plenty of patience. The best players know when to aim right at the hole and when to play it safe to avoid trouble. Consider the following golf aiming tips for the mental side of the game before playing your next round.

Know your own style. Some golfers – and some people in general – are more comfortable taking on risk than others. Which category do you fall into? Do you love taking a gamble from time to time, or are you a 'play it safe kind of person? There is no wrong answer, but you need to be honest with yourself and play the style of golf that best suits you. If you are more comfortable playing the percentages and avoiding trouble, don't try to force yourself to hit risky shots. Pretending to be something you're not will never end well on the golf course. Think about what style of play will suit you best and then pick targets that match that style.

Pick your spots. Before starting a round, look over the scorecard and evaluate where you can afford to take some chances, and where you should be more conservative. Typically, par fives are great places to be aggressive and try to make a birdie – while long par threes and tough par fours call for conservative targets that improve your chances of escaping with a par. Playing aggressive on every single hole all round long isn't likely to be a successful strategy. At the same time, be conservative on all of your shots will limit your ability to lower your scores. Plan out your round ahead of time so you know when you are going to be aggressive and when you are going to play it safe.

Trust your instincts. You might find during a round that you encounter a shot you just don't feel comfortable with. For whatever reason, you don't have confidence that you can hit a good shot from where your ball is positioned. When that happens, take a more conservative line and keep your ball safely away from trouble. Don't fight your gut feeling – if you lack confidence in a certain shot, playing safe is the way to go. On the other side of the coin, you might find a different shot later in the round that fills you with confidence even though there is trouble lurking near the target. In that case, it might be worth the risk to trust your instinct and pick an aggressive target.

Respect the wind. Many golfers fail to consider the wind conditions when they are picking a target for a given shot. If you are playing on a windy day, you should always consider playing toward a safer target simply because you will have less control over the flight of the ball than when playing in calm conditions. A green that might be easy to hit when there is no wind can suddenly become a serious challenge if the breeze picks up. Adjust your targets to account for the wind and understand that you will have to be patient in order to shoot a good score.

Learning how to aim the golf club at address is a skill that every player should work on developing. The best swing in the world isn't going to do you much good if you fail the aim of the club accurately at the target you have picked for the shot. Fortunately, the good aim is one of the easier parts of the game, so long as you follow a specific process like the one laid out above. Have a plan, work on your routine on the practice range, and start aiming at the target more consistently than ever before.

CHAPTER 10: "MISALIGNED" TEE BOXES

I t's nice when golf course designers "aim" tee boxes directly at the center of the fairway or, on par 3s, at the green. But many times the architect, or the superintendent in charge of mowing patterns, will point the tee at an angle to the direction you want to hit the shot – sometimes into the rough, trees, or other trouble.

If you've experienced this, you know that it can add difficulty to lining up correctly. Even when you know the direction of the target, once you stand over the ball your natural tendency is to align the body with the position of the tee markers or the direction of the mowed grass. Other times we manage to line up correctly, but subconsciously swing in the direction that feels correct – e.g. where the tee points – but turns out to be off-target.

Since it's difficult to overcome the sensation that cross-tee alignment causes, you must be absolutely convinced that your aim is correct before addressing the ball.

That's the only way to make a committed, confident swing.

Use this alignment procedure, popularized by Jack Nicklaus.

Stand behind the ball looking straight at the target.

Find an object, such as a broken tee or divot, lying directly on the line between ball and target, no more than a couple of feet in front of your ball.

Step to the ball and line up the clubface precisely with the object.

Take your stance, making sure the clubface remains pointed at the object.

Look at the target for a little longer than usual to gain a visual sense of its position.

Return your eyes to the ground and track the line from your club to the target. This will tell you that you are, in fact, aligned correctly.

Make your swing.

Again, the key is to gain total trust in your aim before taking the club back. You must eliminate doubt and indecision, which will cause you to adjust your alignment and/or swing path to one that feels right, but isn't.

Dealing with Misaligned Tee Boxes

When you start to think about everything that you have to deal with on the golf course, it is amazing that anyone ever makes it from the first hole to the last with a good score. There are so many things that can go wrong along the way, and so many things that you need to know in order to avoid disaster. Just knowing the basic swing technique isn't nearly enough to play good golf – you have to have a bank of knowledge in your mind that you can call on in order to navigate your way through the various problems that are going to come up at one point or another. From weather and poor lies to slow play, fatigue, and much more, you have to be prepared for everything if you want to be a consistent, quality player.

It is with that background in mind that we start to discuss the topic of misaligned tee boxes. This is one of those things that goes into the category of small details on the course that can make a big difference. At first thought, it might not seem like a misaligned tee box could cause much of a problem in your game. However, when you look closer, you see that this really is a big issue. Most golfers simply trust that the tee boxes are aligned with the middle of the fairways – when they aren't, those assumptions are incorrect and the ball is likely to wind up anywhere but the short grass.

Before getting too far into this subtle but important topic, we should first define what is meant by a 'misaligned' tee box. When a tee box is aligned properly, the box itself is in a position that is square to the middle of the fairway (or the green, on a par three). Most tee boxes are either square or rectangular in shape, and most course designers do their best to keep them square to the target as an aid to golfers.

However, that doesn't always happen. Some lower-end golf courses fail to get their tee boxes aligned properly during design, and others fall out of square with the rest of the course as things change over time. For instance, mowing patterns and maintenance could potentially take a tee box out of alignment, even if it was nicely square when the course was built.

The big problem that golfers face when they walk onto a tee that is misaligned is the fact that most players just expect tee boxes to be square. Without even thinking twice, some players will tee the ball up, aim in general alignment with the tee box itself, and swing away. If the box was squared up properly, this isn't a problem. However, if the tee box is out of alignment, even a good swing will send the ball into the rough – or worse.

Any swing instruction included below has been written from the perspective of a right-handed golfer. If you happen to play left-handed, please take a moment to reverse the directions as necessary.

Taking No Chances

When you walk onto a tee box, you could choose to just assume that the tee box is square to the fairway – or you could take a couple of seconds to find out for yourself. Most of the tee boxes that you play will in fact be in a square position, but some will not – meaning you can't take anything for granted. Don't assume that the tee box is leading you in the right direction. It won't take long to find out for sure, and your game will be better off for the effort.

To get a good look at the overall layout of the tee box – and the rest of the hole – the best thing you can do is to stand back a few yards behind the tee markers, looking down the fairway. From this perspective, you will be able to see the shape of the tee box, the position of the tee markers themselves, and the location of your target for the shot. Without doing anything else, you should instantly get a good idea of whether or not the tee box is, in fact, aligned correctly with the target you will be using.

Once you get into the habit of looking over the hole from this perspective, you will find that it simply becomes part of your shot preparation as you begin each hole. When you park your cart or walk up with your bag, take a route that leads you to the back of the tee box before going anywhere else. By planning your movement around the course to include a view from this perspective, you won't have to take any extra time (or spend any extra energy) trying to get a good look at the tee and the target. You will often see experienced golfers taking this kind of route as they walk the golf course, and that isn't by accident. Knowing where to walk is a skill that you can develop over time, and you want to make sure that you include the back of the tee box as one of your top destinations.

You should be using this vantage point on every hole that you play, not just on the par fours and fives. While tee box misalignment doesn't tend to be as much of a problem on par threes – since you are locking in on the hole location during the aiming process – you should still double-check to make sure the tee box doesn't lead you astray. Playing well on a regular basis is all about consistency, and taking a look down the hole from the same perspective each time is just another layer of consistency that you can build into your game.

Picking Your Own Target

Every shot that you hit during a round of golf – with no exceptions – needs a specific target. Whether you are standing on the tee, in the fairway, in the rough, or even on the green, you need to have a very specific target in mind for all shots that you strike. Golf is a target game, so it would be foolish to hit a shot without first selecting a target. By taking the task of picking a target seriously, you can go a long way toward eliminating the concern of tee box misalignment.

One of the common mistakes that are made by the average golfer is assuming that the middle of the fairway is automatically the target for their tee shots. Often, the middle of the fairway will in fact be the right target, but that isn't always the case. Sometimes, you will want to aim down one side or another to play away from a hazard that is lurking.

Or, you may decide to play away from the middle in order to setup a better angle for your next shot. Whatever the case, it is important to think about exactly where you want to place your ball with your tee shot. Making assumptions in golf is always a recipe for trouble, so don't just blindly swing away for the middle of the short grass. Take a moment to pick your target, and be confident in your selection once it is made.

Now that you have a specific target in mind, the next step in the process is to align yourself with that target. This is where a poorly aligned tee box can potentially cause trouble. You need to make sure the process of aligning your stance prior to the swing is based solely on the target itself – not on the orientation of the tee box. To do this successfully, you are going to use what is known as an 'intermediate target'. This is a point that is between your ball and the actual target which you are going to use for alignment purposes. To use an intermediate target successfully, follow the simple steps below –

To start, stand behind your ball on an extension of the target line. From this position, you should be able to look straight up from your ball to find the target. In addition to allowing you to get a good look at the target, this position is also a great place from which to start your pre-shot routine.

While standing behind the ball, look at the ground roughly a foot or so in front of the ball to pick out a spot that is going to serve as your intermediate target. This spot should stand out from the rest of the grass, and it should be easy to identify when you walk up to take your stance. It may be a blade of grass that is discolored, or a leaf, small stone, or just about anything else that grabs your eye. Of course, this object should be perfectly on the line between your ball and the target.

Now that you have your spot picked out, the next thing to do is walk up to the ball and take your stance. The first part of your address position that should be put into place is the club it-self – you should place the clubhead behind the ball before you put your feet into position. Don't look up at your actual target during this phase of the setup. Instead, just look back and forth between your clubface and the intermediate target that you are using for the shot. As long as the clubface is square to that target, you are ready to go.

The clubface should be the basis for everything else that you do in your stance. Once it is in position, make sure it stays per-fectly still while you put together the rest of your stance. When complete, you should feel balanced and athletic while know-ing that the clubface is pointed directly at the target you have picked out for the shot. With the assurance that you are aimed in the right direction, you can now make your swing with total confidence.

When you go through this kind of process prior to hitting your tee shots, you really won't have to worry about misaligned tee boxes. The process you are now using will help you get lined up just right even if the tee box is turned to the right or left signifi-cantly. Work on the process outlined above during your next visit to the driving range in order to get comfortable with it before heading out onto the course. As long as you trust the pro-cess and block out everything else, the alignment of the tee box under your feet will not make any difference to the outcome of your shots.

Dealing With the Par Threes

When you come up to a par three that has a tee box that is

poorly aligned to the green, you will be well-served to stick with the process outlined in the section above. No matter what kind of shot you are facing, going through the process of picking out an intermediate target is a great way to block out all other distractions. However, when it comes to tee shots on par three holes, there are a few specific points that you need to keep in mind with regard to your aim.

Quite obviously, hitting your tee shot on a par three is just like hitting your approach shot on a par four, with the exception of the tee that is sitting beneath your ball. You are playing a shot into a putting surface, and you need to think strategically in order to place your ball in the right spot too – hopefully – setup a birdie putt. Although many golfers like to play them because they don't have to worry about hitting a tee shot with their driver, par threes are actually some of the hardest holes on the course. They are frequently rather long, requiring you to hit a longer iron than you would hit on a typical approach shot for a par four or par five. If you would like to make sure you aim intelligently on the par threes, even when the tee box is misaligned, use the list of tips below.

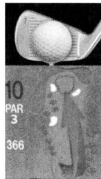

Play for the low side. This is a tip that very few golfers understand, let alone actually put into use, but it is one of the best ways to lower your scores on par three holes. When standing on the tee, take a look at the hole location compared to the topography of the course on and around the green. Where is the low side of the hole? If there is a significant slope in play, you always want to favor your shots toward the low side. Playing your second shot uphill – whether you are putting or chipping – is going to give you a great advantage over having to play downhill. You can easily make a bogey or worse when playing from the high side, so do your best to get the ball below the hole whenever possible.

Fire away with shorter clubs. As mentioned above, many par three holes feature significant yardage, meaning you will be happy just to get the ball on the green at all. However, for those par three holes that do give you a chance to play from inside of 150 or so, you should be taking dead aim at the pin. Since you are able to tee the ball up, there should be no trouble getting your shot up in the air and on line with a short iron. There is never anything wrong with making a par on a par three, but you can feel free to go after a birdie when the yardage is on the shorter side.

Avoid unnecessary risks. One of the worst things you can do on a par three is to make a big mistake from the tee that will cost you several strokes before the hole is completed. Avoid taking on too much risk by playing safely away from any hazards that are guarding the green. Specifically, pay attention to water hazards that are in play. When you hit the ball in the water on a par three, you will often be left with very few good options in terms of a drop location. It is common to have a water ball turn into a double or triple bogey on a par three. Be smart, be patient, and play to the safe side of the hole when a hazard is in play.

You will likely run into more than a few tee boxes which are misaligned on par threes if you play a variety of courses over the years to come. However, if you think more about the tips above than you do about the tee box itself, you should be just fine. Remember, once you have decided on a target for your shot, use the intermediate target method to align yourself perfectly before you make a swing.

Rising Above the Course

The issue of misaligned tee boxes leads nicely into another, bigger, issue that has been known to plague the average golfer. When struggling during a round, many golfers are prone to blame the golf course itself, rather than looking at their own performance for the cause of the struggles. You might recognize this pattern in your game from time to time.

For instance, have you ever tried to blame the green for a missed putt, when it was really you who pulled the ball to the left? Or, have you cursed the ground for giving your ball a firm bounce over the green when you should have known that the turf was going to be firm? All golfers are guilty of this kind of attitude from time to time – but if you wish to be a better player, you need to rise above it and take ownership of your game.

In the end, the golf course doesn't care how you play, or how you score. It isn't 'out to get you', or anything like that. The course is what it is, and it isn't going to change when your shots are hit. Don't think about the course as your enemy so much as you think about it as an obstacle course. You need to plan your way around the course using all of the information you have available, including what you can see in front of you, what you have learned from past shots, and more. The more information you include in your decision-making process when planning a shot, the better chance you will have to succeed.

This is the way you should think about the topic of misaligned tee boxes. Can they be annoying? Sure. Do they have the potential to lead you astray? Of course. However, if you do your job correctly – meaning, you do a good job of picking a target and aiming at that target accurately – you should have nothing to worry about. It is certainly possible to hit great drives from misaligned tees, as long as you focus on the details without getting too caught up in the overall shape and direction of the teeing ground itself. You could take the easy way out and blame the course for your poor shots, but that really wouldn't help you play any better. If you are serious about shooting lower scores, you will drop any kind of excuse you may have and instead focus your attention on hitting better shots and playing better golf.

Golf courses aren't perfect. Unlike other sports, which have perfectly square and parallel lines to mark out the playing surface, golf is played over thousands of yards of imperfect earth. There are going to be all kinds of bumps, divots, bare spots, and much more along the route. No matter what you encounter, including misaligned tee boxes, you are tasked with the job of keeping your focus and making great swings to specific targets from the first hole on through to the last.

CHAPTER 11: SOLID CONTACT

"**K**eep your eye on the ball." it's a cliché used in most sports, and golf is no exception.

It certainly makes sense that you must be looking at the golf ball in order to hit it. But it helps to zero in on the exact part of the ball you want to strike – in every case except greenside bunker shots, that means focusing on the back of the ball.

Your gaze should remain fixed on that spot from the takeaway to the top of the backswing and into impact. Try to keep the eyes focused there until the golf ball has been struck, letting them follow the shot naturally as the head moves left and up in the follow-through.

In maintaining focus on the back of the ball, one shouldn't allow the neck and head to become rigid. Making a full, easy-flowing backswing requires the head to turn slightly with the shoulders. Attempting to keep the head perfectly still introduces tension, shortening the backswing and robbing the player of distance.

One other eye-related note: Many right-handed golfers tend to aim right of the target, while lefties aim left. This is because the eye farthest from the target skews the appearance of the line to the right-handers right (or the left-handers left). Clubs with built-in alignment aids can help overcome this tendency.

Use Your Eyes Right to Play Better Golf

Your eyes aren't going to ever touch your golf club during the swing, but they are one of the most important tools you have available to play better golf. The best players in the world understand how to control their eye movements to ensure that they are looking at the right things at the right time. When you let your eyes wander in directions that aren't helpful to your game, you are wasting an opportunity to gather information. Have a plan for where you are going to look both before and during your swing, and then execute that plan when you get out onto the course.

Out of all of the parts of your body that you have to be worried about during the swing – your legs, your arms, your hands, etc. – it wouldn't seem like your eyes would enter into the equation. Shouldn't you just be able to look at the ball while making your swing? Well yes, looking at the ball during your swing is a great place to start. Unfortunately, it isn't quite that simple during the rest of the time you spend on the course. Only a couple minutes total within a four hour round are spend making a swing – the rest of the time is spent walking around and preparing for your shots. It is during those times that you need to know where to look, and why. Making the most of the non-swing time that you have on the course will allow you to perform better when you actually are making your swings.

One of the big problems that golfers run into when trying to control how they use their eyes on the course is a distraction. Most golf courses have plenty to distract you during a round, whether it is other golfers, scenery, or even traffic driving by. To play your best, you will need to learn to block out those distractions and focus your vision on the important parts of the course. Any time spent looking off into the distance at a tree or another golfer is time you could have spent preparing yourself to play the best shot possible with your next swing. You don't have to stay completely focused for the entire round, but you do need to know when it is okay to be distracted, and when you need to focus on the job at hand.

All of the instruction below is based on a right-handed golfer. If you play golf left-handed, please be sure to reverse the directions as necessary.

How to Use Your Eyes Before a Tee Shot

Hitting a good tee shot is an important step toward making par or better on any given hole. A poor tee shot will put your ball out of position and put you at risk of making a bogey or worse. Therefore, you want to do everything you can to make sure your ball finds the right position in the fairway to setup an easy approach. While making a good swing is key, so too is using your eyes properly before the swing begins.

Below are three keys that you should follow with respect to where your eyes look in the moments leading up to each tee shot that you hit.

Examine the fairway. The first thing you need to do with your eyes prior to a tee shot is to examine the fairway and the hazards around it. Your eyes should be up and looking down the hole from the moment that you arrive on the tee box. Since you will be placing the ball on a tee, you don't need to worry about analyzing the type of lie that you have in this case. Your lie is going to be perfect on the tee, so maintain your focus further down the hole. Things that you should be looking for include any major hazards, the angle and slope of the fairway, and the ideal position to setup your approach shot.

Lookup for the wind. Judging the wind is an important skill for a golfer to have, and your eyes can actually help you make better determinations on wind conditions. If you are playing a tree-lined course, look up to the tops of the trees to see if there is any wind blowing. You might not feel any wind while standing on the tee, but that doesn't mean that it isn't up there waiting to affect your ball. Since your shot will hopefully fly high into the air, you need to analyze the wind conditions aloft rather than on the ground. Use your eyes, and the tops of the trees, to gather this important piece of information.

Take one last look at the target. Once you are standing over your ball, all of the pre-shot preparations should be concluded. You should know what club you are hitting (since you are holding it), and you should have a clear target picked out to guide your swing. As you take your stance, look down at the ball while you put the club into position. Prior to starting your swing, take one last look up at the target that you have selected. Stare at it for just a second or two, then return your gaze back down to the ball. Once your eye refocuses on the ball, start your swing right away. There shouldn't be a delay at this point – allow your eyes to trigger the start of your backswing.

None of these points should be very surprising, and you probably already do most of what is included above in your current golf game. However, your game will benefit if you can get into a consistent habit of using your eyes in this manner each and every time to prepare to hit a tee shot. Consistency is hard to find on the golf course, so building it into your routine is a great way to find more repeatable results. Make sure your eye habits don't change from shot to shot and you can expect your game to quickly improve.

Subtle Changes for Approach Shots

For the most part, the routine that you use for your tee shots is going to be the same as the one you use for your approach shots. You still want to keep your gaze mostly focused down the hole so you can analyze hazards and select a target. However, there are some key differences in the way you should prepare to hit a shot into the green as opposed to when you are hitting one off the tee.

The first difference is the need to analyze the lie of the ball in the grass. When you don't get to tee the ball up, the lie that you have for each shot takes on major importance. If you have a good lie with no long grass around the ball, you should be able to hit just about any type of shot that you wish. That changes when you find your ball in some long grass, or maybe even in an old divot hole. The first thing that you should do when you arrive at your ball looks down at the lie that you have and decide what kind of shots are going to be possible. Only after you have looked carefully at the lie should you move on to other aspects of your pre-shot routine.

Another difference in the way you use your eyes for an approach shot is the need to be as specific as possible with the selection of your target. You should be using your eyes to pick out a very small spot on the green to use as the target for your shot. When playing a tee shot, you might be able to get away with something like the right side of the fairway for a target, but that won't work on an approach.

Look carefully at the green and be as specific as you can before settling on a target that you are comfortable with. This target should allow you the potential to get the ball close to the hole while simultaneously limiting your risk as much as possible. If you have used your eyes correctly and carefully reviewed the entire green complex, it should be easy to settle on a target that feels comfortable and gives you confidence prior to your swing.

One final point that relates to using your eyes during approach shots has to do with what you watch after the ball has been struck. Once the ball leaves your club, there is obviously nothing more you can do to affect the outcome of the shot. You can, however, watch the flight of the ball carefully to gather information for later in the round. Many golfers make the mistake of looking away in frustration before the ball is even halfway to the hole – this habit will cost you an opportunity to learn about your game so you can do better later on. Watch the flight of the ball all the way from the clubface until it lands. Even if this particular shot didn't work out as you had planned, you will now have a better picture in your mind of the ball flight that you are hitting with your irons. Use that information in the planning of your next approach shot, and hopefully, the results will be better.

Managing Eye Movement
During the Swing Itself

The basic advice of keeping your eye on the ball is sound, and most golfers could benefit from following that advice more carefully. When you keep your eye on the ball, you will give yourself the best chance to make solid contact because your head shouldn't be moving around too much during the swing. Keeping your eye on the ball might sound simple, but in practice, it can actually be quite difficult to achieve.

The following are three mistakes that you need to avoid if you are going to be more successful in your effort to keep your eyes on the ball throughout the golf swing.

Don't follow the clubhead in the takeaway. This is a common mistake among many amateur golfers – as soon as the clubhead starts to move back away from the ball, they allow their eyes to follow it for at least the first few inches. This is a problem because it requires the golfer to then refocus their eyes back on the ball at some point during the swing. There is no need to make things more complicated than they have to be by adding this additional step into your technique. Avoid the temptation to watch the clubhead move away from the ball and maintain your focus throughout the swing. It may help to pick out a specific spot on the golf ball such as a dot or another marking that you can use as your focus point.

Don't get anxious. The other common mistake that is made with the eyes during the swing is looking up too early as the club gets down near the impact zone. There is no reason to look up early, as there is nothing you can do once the ball leaves the clubface anyway. Despite that, many golfers are anxious to see where the ball is going so they allow their eyes to leave the ball before impact has actually been reached.

The problem with doing this is that it can have a ripple effect on the rest of your swing. Your eyes moving up will cause your head to move up, which can in turn pull your shoulders up and out of position. Suddenly, your whole upper body will be too high and you are likely to hit the shot thin as a result. Commit to keeping your eyes down and trust that you will be happy with the results of the shot when you finally do a lookup.

Don't get distracted by your shadow. This one only comes into play in certain situations, but it can be a big problem if you let it bother you. When playing on a sunny day, and when the sun is behind you as you take your stance, your shadow will be cast out over the ball. That isn't a big deal – until you start your swing and notice all of the moving parts that are being projected onto the ground. For some golfers, it is a tremendous challenge to ignore the moving shadow and keep looking at the ball throughout the swing.

If you watch your shadow instead of the ball, expect to have trouble making good contact with the shot. To avoid this problem, pay extra attention to your ball at address and make sure you have picked out a specific point on the ball to watch for the duration of the swing. If necessary, try drawing something unique on your golf ball that you can look at while swinging. It will take some practice to learn how to focus despite being distracted by the shadow, so work on this skill on the driving range just like you would any other part of your game.

It sounds easy enough to just keep your eye on the ball during your swing – but experienced golfers know it isn't quite that simple. Avoid making the mistakes above and you should be a big step closer to successfully accomplishing this basic fundamental.

Your Eyes and the Short Game

As important as your eyes are to the long game, they might be even more important when it comes to the short game. When playing short shots around the green, you need to accurately read the ground between you and the hole to analyze break from side to side, determine how hard to hit the shot, etc. Without being able the read the greens properly prior to hitting a short game shot, you will have very little chance of success.

Most average golfers never really learn the right way to use their eyes in the short game, and it shows in the results that they are able to achieve. Chipping and putting are the areas of the game where the typical amateur golfer stands to improve the most – yet those same players tend to spend the majority of their practice time swinging away on the driving range. If you are serious about lower scores, you will dedicate yourself to the short game, and part of mastering the short game is learning how to use your eyes properly.

When you are off the green and playing a chip or a pitch, the first thing you need to do is read the lie of the ball in the grass (just like on an approach shot). Knowing what kind of lie you have will set the stage for the type of shot you are going to choose. For example, if you have a clean lie on short grass, you can try hitting a low chip shot that has plenty of spins to stop it quickly. However, from the deep rough, that shot just isn't an option. Instead, you will need to use loft to stop the ball since the shot is going to have very little backspin out of the rough.

Your eyes will tell you everything you need to know about the lie that you are facing, but it is crucial that you look closely and don't skip this step. Even if you don't know a lot about what the lie can do to your ball at the moment, still make sure to look carefully before each chip or pitch. Over time, you will learn from your experiences and your ability to read the lie will get better and better.

When it comes to putting, your eyes are used to read the break of the putt and pick out the ideal target line. Reading greens is another golf skill that usually develops with experience, but you have to give it your full attention before each and every putt in order to accumulate that knowledge in your mind. If you just walk up to your putts and hit them quickly without giving much thought to the reader, you won't have a chance to develop your visual skills on the green.

Below are some quick tips related to green reading to help you get a jump start on your progress –

Look from both ends. It is important that you read your putts both from behind the ball and from behind the hole. When you look down the line of your putt, it will be far easier to read the end that is closer to you. Therefore, you need to stand behind your ball to read the first half of the putt, and behind the hole to read the finish. Only when you have both perspectives in your mind can you come up with a final read.

Look carefully at the grass itself. Depending on where you play golf, there may be a strong grain in the grass that influences the roll of the ball. This is especially common in areas with warm summers where Bermuda grass is commonly used. Watch for a prevailing grain direction – it often grows toward the setting sun – and account for that in your reader as well.

Look at the big picture. Don't allow your vision to become too focused on just the ground between your ball and the hole. Instead, take a moment and look at the green as a whole to decide which way it is slanted. This perspective can come in handy specifically when you think you have a straight putt. If the putt looks straight, but the green is tilted in one direction as a whole, you might want to play for your putt to break in that same direction.

You can never have too much information when playing golf, and your eyes are the best way to gather that information. Come up with a plan that allows you to look for all of the information you need before each shot and stick with that routine throughout your rounds. Consistently using your eyes the same way round after round is a great way to improve your performance without changing a single thing about your golf swing.

CHAPTER 12: STRONGER GRIP

I fyou have trouble slicing the golf ball, the problem may not be your swing. It could be how you grip the club.

A grip position that is too "weak" – where the hands are rotated to the left of a "neutral" position – the clubface to close on the backswing and open on the downswing, creating a severe left-to-right slice (for right-handers).

To check your grip position, hold a club in your usual manner, and look at the back of your left-hand. If only one knuckle (index finger) is visible, your grip is overly weak. Two knuckles equal a neutral grip; three is strong; four is too strong.

Adjust to a stronger position like this:

Grip the club normally, then relax your hold.

Turn both hands about 1/8 inch to the right.

Note the position of the left knuckles and practice with your new grip. It will take some time to adjust to the feeling, and your shot shape may not change immediately. If you're still slicing after becoming comfortable, continue tweaking in 1/8-inch increments until you achieve a free release of the club.

If you reach the point where three knuckles are visible and your slice hasn't improved, your swing is the likely culprit.

Fix Your Slice With a Stronger Grip?

If you are fighting a slice, you have probably already tried count-less fixes in the hopes of straightening out your ball flight once and for all. It can be difficult to enjoy the game of golf when you consistently see your ball slice off to the right of the target – in fact, some players have given up on the game altogether after being unable to fix their slice successfully. However, that does not have to be the case for you. As surprising as it might be, fixing your slice could come down to a simple grip change. By moving your grip into a stronger position at address, you may be able to correct the underlying issues that are creating the slice.

The grip that you use on the club at the address has a powerful influence over the shots you are able to hit as you make your way around the course. A quality grip is one that compliments that swing you are trying to make. Unfortunately, many ama-teur golfers use a grip that runs counter to their intended swing, meaning they are fighting against their grip each time they hit a shot. Golf is a hard enough game on its own – you don't need to make it harder by working against your own grip time after time.

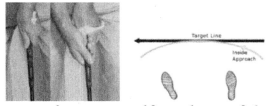

One of the reasons that many golfers who are fighting the slice never think to make a grip adjustment is the simple fact that it is difficult to get used to a new grip. When you do make a grip change, those first few shots are awkward at best – and down-right uncomfortable at worst. You have to have the patience to see your grip change through to the end if you are going to wind up with improved results. While you might see minor improvements in your ball flight right away, the real reward is only going to come after plenty of practice, both on the driving range and on the course. It is certainly possible to make a successful grip change, but you should not count on it happening overnight.

Even though it may take some time, it is certainly worth your effort to look into using a grip change to solve your slice. Many players never manage to get over the problem of the slice, forever playing from the right side of the golf course (for a right-handed player). You might be able to 'learn to live' with your slice as you play the game, but you will never have the potential to dramatically lower your scores if you always have to accommodate a big slice on each of your long shots. By taking the time now to work on eliminating that slice once and for all, you can give yourself a chance to enjoy the game at a higher level for many years to come.

All of the content below is based on a right-handed golfer. If you happen to play left-handed, please take a moment to reverse the directions as necessary.

What is a Stronger Grip?

There seems to be a fair amount of confusion among amateur golfers as to what is really meant by the term 'stronger grip'. To the non-golfer, a stronger grip would seem to indicate one where the player squeezes more-tightly onto the handle of the club. That, of course, is not the case. Rather, a strong grip refers to the positioning of your hands on the club. Players who use a strong grip have their left-hand turned farther to the right on the top of the grip, while those using a weak grip have that left-hand turned farther to the left. It is possible to play good golf using either option, but players who are fighting a slice will almost always benefit by moving in a stronger direction.

Of course, you can't really make your grip stronger if you are already in a strong position, so the first step in this process is to evaluate the current status of your grip. To do so, follow the simple steps below –

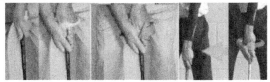

Take any one of your full swing clubs (not your putter) from the bag and get into a normal stance as if you were going to hit a standard shot. You aren't going to swing the club at all in this process, but you should still take the time to build a proper stance.

With your stance taken, drop your right-hand off of the club so that your left-hand is holding the club still in the address position.

Look down at the back of your left-hand – how many knuckles can you see? The number of knuckles you can count on the back of your left-hand will indicate how strong (or weak) your grip is at the moment.

If you can see just one or two knuckles, you are using a weak grip and your slice can probably be improved by adjusting into a stronger position. However, if you can see three or even four knuckles, you are already using a strong grip and you will probably need to look elsewhere for changes that can eliminate your slice. It is important that you take the time to do this quick evaluation as you don't want to try making a strong grip even stronger – you could harm your swing and cause even more problems in your game. Go through this quick check and only proceed with the rest of the instruction in this chapter if you are, indeed, using a weak grip in your current swing.

The Benefits

There are a number of ways in which using a stronger grip can help you to avoid the slice pattern that has been giving you trouble in your game. Since your grip is the only connection you have between your body and the club itself, it is important that you position your hands in a way that is going to cause the club to do the right things. Even a great golf swing can be ruined by a poor grip – and a so-so swing can actually lead to quality results as long as the hands are positioned properly on the club.

So, how can using a stronger grip help you to steer clear of the slice? Consider the following points.

Easier release. This is really the key point related to using a stronger grip, and it is the reason you may be able to improve your slice by making this change. When your left-hand is in a stronger position on the top of the grip, you will find it easier to release the clubhead through the hitting area. Most players who fight a slice never really manage to release the club properly – and if they do, that release takes place too late. With a strong grip, your left-hand will have a much easier time achieving the release, meaning you should be able to get the clubface back to the square in time to avoid a dramatic slice. Even if you still hit a bit of a fade, your ball flight pattern should be improved thanks to this adjustment.

Better takeaway path. By moving your left-hand into a stronger position, you will be more likely to take the club back away from the ball on a better path. Those who play with a weak grip are prone to moving the club outside of the target line early in the backswing – which can wind up leading to an outside-in impact path in the end. With your strong grip in place, all you will need to do is turn your shoulders away from the target in order to trace an appropriate path back from the ball. While many golfers think of the slice as a downswing problem, it often is caused by a faulty takeaway. Move your grip into a stronger position and the takeaway that has been giving you problems could soon be far more effective.

Hold your lag. This point goes along with the previous point relating to the release. When you use a stronger grip, you may find it easier to hold your lag on the way down toward the ball – which is a key in hitting straight, powerful shots. Most amateur golfers struggle to hold on to their leg during the downswing, which is why they don't tend to hit the ball as far as their professional counterparts. Moving your grip into a stronger position won't automatically allow you to use lag more effectively in the downswing, but it certainly will be a good start.

Stability through the hitting area. Not surprisingly, a stronger grip will help you hold the clubface in a steady position through impact. Players with a weak grip often allow the club to twist at impact when the ball is not quite struck on the center of the face – but that is not a problem usually encountered by players with a strong left-hand position. Not only can the ability to hold the face steady help you in terms of preventing the slice pattern from taking over your game, but it will also help you to play better from poor lies, such as when the ball is sitting down in the rough.

Playing with a strong grip is a great idea for many players, even if they don't struggle with a slice. However, for those who do need to find a way to get rid of the slice, using a strong grip is almost a no-brainer. There are plenty of benefits, and few (if any) drawbacks to speak of with this technique. A great number of players in the professional ranks play with a strong grip, which should be all the proof you need that it is possible to take your game to a high level by employing this technique.

To provide both sides of the story on the matter of a strong grip, it is only fair to point out the potential minor drawbacks that can be experienced. In some cases, using a strong grip will make the player prone to hitting a quick hook, especially if the player allows their lower body to stop moving through the downswing. However, since you are working on fixing your slice at the moment, there is almost no chance that you are going to run into problems with the hook.

Also, for some players, the strong grip will make it difficult to hit down through iron shots properly. The improved release that comes along with this kind of grip can potentially cause the club to shallow out early, leading to an impact that is flatter than desired. Again, this is a problem that will only affect a small portion of players, and it is an issue that can be dealt with by making a couple of other adjustments.

In all, it is hard to find too much bad to say about the strong grip. For most amateur players, experimenting with a strong grip is a smart move, as there is plenty to be gained and very little to be lost. Even if you don't wind up sticking with the strong grip over the long run, the practice time spent working on this technique will still help you in your pursuit of a slice-free future.

Making the Change

As was mentioned above, making a grip change is one of the trickiest things you can do in the game of golf. You are used to the feeling that your current grip provides during the swing, so making a chance to a new grip position is going to dramatically alter the whole feel of your motion. Of course, you can't make progress without going through a period of adjustment, so you will need to accept the fact that you are going to have to put up with some uncomfortable swings before you can make the strong grip a natural part of your technique.

To start making this change, the best thing you can do is spend plenty of time working on your short game. That's right – even though you are trying to fix the slice that occurs when you take a full swing, the first place you want to head when making a grip change is the short game practice area. Why? To start to develop a level of comfort with the feel of your new grip. Hitting chip and pitch shots is like making miniature full swings, so you can build up comfort and confidence at this level before gradually working your way up to full swings with long clubs.

Take one of your wedges from the bag and hit as many chip and pitch shots as you would like with your new, stronger grip. At first, this is going to feel uncomfortable even with a short swing. Do get over your discomfort, focus your mind on the task of hitting the ball cleanly each time. Don't worry too much about how it feels at this point – just think about putting the sweet spot of the club on the back of the ball. Spend as much time as possible over the first few days of this change hitting chip and pitch shots with your lofted clubs.

As you gain confidence, gradually start to work your way into longer and longer shots. Pretty soon you will find that your pitch shots are turning into half-swings, and those half-swings will then turn into full golf swings. By building up in this way, you can almost 'trick' yourself into being comfortable with your new grip. Of course, as an added bonus, you will have spent plenty of time working on your short game, which is never a bad thing.

It is common to make the mistake of gripping the club too tightly while working on a grip change, so watch out for that issue as you move along. Your grip pressure should always be relatively light, as a light grip will make it easier for the club to swing freely through the hitting area. You need to have enough pressure on the club to keep it under control, of course, but you should never feel like you are squeezing as tight as you can during the swing. This is another reason why it is a good idea to start with short game shots before moving into full swing. Using light grip pressure on short game shots is easy, so get comfortable using the right amount of pressure when pitching the ball and then monitor that point as you add more and more speed to your shots.

The biggest hurdle in this entire process is simply getting out of your own way. You will likely be uncomfortable with the new grip in the early stages, so you will be tempted to move back into a weaker grip just to get back to a point that feels comfortable to you. That would be a mistake, and it would mean you would have to resign to many more months or years of hitting a slice. Stick with this process even through the tough times at the start, and look for minor signs of improvement along the way to keep you motivated.

Taking It To The Course

You might be thinking that shooting a good score will be no problem at all once you have eliminated your slice through the use of a stronger grip. While it will be easier to post good scores when you hit the ball straighter, it might not quite be the 'walk in the park' that you are expecting. Why? It comes down to learning how to play a new game. If you have been dealing with a slice for some time, you have adapted your game to accommodate that left-to-right ball flight. Even though it wasn't ideal, you learned how to score your best by playing for your slice in most cases. Now, you don't need to play for the slice anymore, but your body may not be adjusted to that new reality.

The first thing you will need to change is your alignment at address. Most players who slice learn how to aim out to the left of the target in order to give the ball room to curve back toward the fairway or the green. Of course, now that you aren't slicing the ball, that kind of adjustment is not necessary. You will be able to aim much closer to the target, although you will still want to aim slightly to one side or another to account for your new ball flight (hopefully either a small draw or small fade). To get your aim right, you need to pay attention to the pre-shot process that you use to get ready for your shots. Pick out a very specific target, align your body and the club to that target, and then make a quality swing.

Once you have learned how to aim properly with your new ball flight, the other change you will have to make is to the strategy that you use around the course. Most likely, you have taught yourself to be scared of hazards that lurk on the right side of the golf course, as you would have had trouble avoiding those spots with your slice. Now, you no longer need to play with that fear, as you should be able to keep your ball safely away from the right side when needed. It can take some time to 'recalibrate' the way you think about the game, so pay attention to your course management decisions until you get familiar with play-ing without a slice.

It is hard to have very much fun on the golf course while fighting a slice. Countless golfers deal with the slice each time they tee it up, and those players are unable to move their scores lower as a result. By working on using a stronger grip in your swing, you just might be able to break free of the slice pattern that has been following you throughout much of your golf career. Good luck, and hit 'em straight!

CHAPTER 13: ARMS ALIGNMENT

The arms dictate much of what happens in the golf swing. They influence swing plane, arc, width, path, and, well, just about everything in one way or another.

Therefore, it's important to begin the swing with your arms properly positioned.

Perhaps the most common mistake among amateurs is extending the arms too far from the body or reaching for the ball. Some players feel this gives them more power, but it can actually drain clubhead speed by altering your posture and causing upper-body tension.

Instead, let the arms hang naturally from the shoulders. This goes hand in hand with developing the correct spine angle and allowing your body to rotate freely back and through.

Be careful not to pull the arms too close to the body, as you'll restrict the backswing turn and force the club over-the-top on the downswing.

Here's a tip that'll help you get into a proper setup position:

Address the Ball at the Perfect Distance

Here are a few more tips for arranging your arms just right:

The left-arm should form a straight (or nearly straight) line with the shaft, from shoulder to ball.

The right arm should be tension-free; a little bend at the elbow is OK.

Viewed from your right looking toward the target, the left arm should appear slightly higher than the right.

If the left arm is level with or beneath the right arm, your shoulders are probably open to the target line (aiming left). If the left arm is much higher than the right, your shoulders are closed.

One oft-cited rule states that the hands should be about one palm's width from your body (about 4 in – 6 in) when setting up to a short or mid-iron, and a bit farther for long irons, hybrids, and woods.

If your shots lack power and accuracy, check your arms along with fundamentals like alignment, grip, posture, and ball position. The answer – and the cure – often lies in the setup.

Golf Arms at Address:

The arms are like the rubber band in a slingshot. Pull them back to the correct position and let them fly! First, however, make sure the arms are in a position to soar, not suppress. In golf, the address is the most important and controllable part of the swing.

At address, the arms should be in a position to allow a bit of arm swing during the takeaway before the shoulders and chest even start to turn. As the arms start to swing, the left arm will create a connection with your chest. To make sure your arms work correctly during the takeaway, do this drill ensures your distance from the ball and posture are not hindering your ability to create an arm swing.

Without a club in your hands, bend over into your golf posture.

With your hands hanging down separately, swing your left arm across the chest and under the right arm.

If your chest and arm move back together it's because your upper left arm is already connected at address, you are too close to the ball or your knees are bent too much.

If your left arm swings back and doesn't connect to the chest then you are too far away from the ball or too bent over.

Remember that connection can be created by either the bicep or the triceps connecting with the chest. It depends on your chest size and flexibility which is used. For women many times you are using your triceps to connect because your left arm should start on top of your chest at address.

Your grip will be dependent on how your arms hang. If you start with your left arm on top of your chest then you should have a strong left-hand. For the right-hand grip, get into your golf address position and take your right-hand off of the club. It should be easy to place the right-hand back on the club in the position it is hanging from.

If your left arm is starting from the side of your chest, your left-hand should be slightly stronger than neutral. Again, let the right arm hang and then grip the club as it hangs. As your left arm connects to your chest on the takeaway, several things happen. First, your right arm will begin to fold. If your right arm is too far behind you as it folds, checks your right-hand grip to make sure that it is not too strong. An early fold won't work well for players that have a one-piece takeaway.

The left-arm connection also forces the left arm to rotate. If the left arm rotates too quickly and pushes your left arm away from your chest then you might have too much knee bend. This will cause your upper body to be too upright and prevent any kind of arm swing. Next, the hang of your arms and the resulting grip will now need to be matched with your ball position. Your ball position should work in harmony with your grip and arms to allow proper release. If you have a strong left-hand grip the ball should be closer to the middle of your stance. A strong grip will cause the club to release sooner.

If your grip is neutral, the ball position should be opposite the left side of your nose and if you have a one-piece takeaway the ball should be placed opposite your left cheek. Finally, when addressing the ball it is important that your elbows relax down towards your hips. If the elbows point out during the swing it makes a difference in your release. For instance, if your left elbow is too low going back it makes the right elbow point out. During the downswing, the left elbow will point out and high. This delays your release and creates what some people call a chicken wing.

Setting up with your arms in the proper positions will have a direct effect on the impact and your release point. Take time to examine your golf arms at the address and set them up for success in your golf swing!

Golf Arms at Impact Indicate
Efficiency of Your Swing

The golf swing is a sequence of events, but more importantly, the golf swing is dynamic. The significance of your arms at impact is important because the golf club is acting as an extension of your arms while the body is in motion.

Here are some things that we already know about the arms and how they should be working at impact:

1.The left arm is nearly straight.

2.The right arm is slightly bent.

3.The elbows are pointed downward.

4.The upper arms should be connected to the torso.

These two drills will help you evaluate where your arms are at impact. Both encourage motion in the swing while highlighting your golf arms at impact.

IMPACT BAG DRILL

This aid is basically a heavy bag of towels or rags. The resistance of the bag stops you at impact.

You can look down and see where your arms are when you hit the bag. This is one of the best teaching aids made for position people. While evaluating your arms you can see your clubface position, hand placement, and body location.

IMPACT TRIGGER DRILL

Use this drill to setup where you aspire to be an impact.

setup in your normal address position.

Turn your hips slightly towards the target while keeping the upper body pointing at the ball.

Allow the hands to push forward a little bit, so they are ahead of the ball and the shaft is bending back from top to bottom. Take a picture in your mind of how this feels.

Turn back to your normal address position then swing.

If your ball flight is not as you intended it to be, ask yourselves some questions:

Where did the ball start and where did it trend to at the end of the ball's flight?

Did you hit the ball cleanly or was it a thin or fat shot?

Did you hit the ball towards the heel or toe of the clubface?

If you go back to what we know the arms SHOULD be doing at impact, those things should help you figure out your troubles. For instance, if the shot felt fat or thin, look to see if your arms are bent too much at impact. A thin shot might come from the arms not being extended enough. This can happen if you are trying to prevent the clubface from closing or if your body is moving towards the ground on the downswing.

Your mind can sense that you are going to hit the ground too hard and instinctively your arms will bend. A tell-tale sign would be that one of your elbows is pointing out rather than down. If your arms release too soon on the downswing you most likely will hit behind the ball. Your arms should be slightly bent at impact so if they are straight you have already released any power you might have had. You will also be swinging down to the ball in a shallow angle of attack. In another example, if your arms do not follow your shoulder line and do not stay in front of your chest, then most likely you will be looking at off-center hits and exaggerated shots to the left and right.

Most likely your impact position would look like you have already released your lower body and your shoulders. The arms would appear to be lagging behind. The impact is only one point in time during the length of a golf swing. It's a place of measurement and the one position that will give you insight into the entirety of your swing. Use your impact position to aid you in discovering what might be happening during your swing up to that point. Your arms will be good indicators as to how efficient they and the body have been working together.

Golf Arms Connected to the Body

Whenever I think of the connection of the arms to the body I think of Top 100 Teacher Jimmy Ballard and the distinctive golf swing that he teaches. Ballard talks about laying the left arm on top of the shoulder girdle and keeping it there the entire swing. He even goes as far as saying that both arms should stay connected at ALL times, which is the feature that makes his student's swings so remarkable.

Connection affects your plane, clubface position, power, and release point.

During the golf swing your arms provide:

CONNECTIONThe upper left arm in contact with the torso.

ELEVATIONFolding the right arm elevates the golf club.

COIL-Stretching the left shoulder so that the left arm's connection helps pull the left shoulder back tightly.

SUPPORT -The right arm supports the golf club during the swing to prevent the club from experiencing unwanted motion.

RELEASESince the right arm folds in the backswing creating a lever, it can straighten on the downswing creating a release.

The connection is what makes elevation, coil, support, and release work more smoothly.

After your left arm connects to your chest on the takeaway, several things happen. First, your right arm will begin to fold. As the right arm folds, it begins to support the golf club and rotate the left arm. Ideally, if your right arm supports the club correctly it will help you stay on plane. Keeping control of the club and maintaining connections will help produce coil. When tension builds then it also has to release. The coil will assist the arms in straightening down to the ball without feeling you need to throw your hands down.

Right arm connection is good for some on the backswing, but for power, our right arm needs to be disconnected from your body on the backswing so that you can have space to drop your arms on the downswing. You can actually be over-connected with the right arm. On the downswing, your right arm should drop because while the arms are still finishing the backswing the hips start the downswing. At that point, both arms should be connected to your chest until after impact.

Here are some examples of how your left arm might lose connection:

Standing too tall or too close to the ball will force the upper left arm off of the chest and the club will swing behind you.

If the right arm is too low in the backswing, the left arm will be too high and force the left arm off of the chest.

Over-swinging the arms in the backswing will force the left arm off of the chest.

If the club falls behind the hands on the downswing the left arm will come up off of the chest.

If your spine angle dips to the right on the downswing it will make the left arm lift off of the chest.

The right arm can over-connect on backswing anytime the left arms lose connection. If you have a very strong right-hand grip it also can cause the right elbow to pull back and connect too soon. Evaluate your swing to discover if the arm connection is working to your advantage. The easiest way to see if you have a connection leak is to place a headcover under your left armpit and swing. If the headcover stays in place until the post-impact position you should be fine. To stop over the connection of the right arm place a golf ball under your right armpit and release the ball on the backswing.

Golf Arms Connected to the Body mean power, efficiency, and accuracy. Connect with your swing!

In Golf Right Arm Close to Body Means Power in Your Swing

It has long been stated in golf that a power swing move is to tuck your right arm in on the downswing. However, if there isn't a lot of width between the elbow and body when you start your downswing, many times the golf club will get stuck behind you.

Your right elbow bends during the backswing. If you want to support the club as you swing back, the elbow will separate itself from the chest. The more separation you can achieve on the backswing, the more space your right arm will have to drop towards the body on the downswing. The easiest way to think of this concept is to think you are swinging your right arm from wide to narrow.

Let's assume that you have made a good backswing and not only does your right arm have width, it's in a good position to support the golf club. As the arms complete the backswing, the hips will start moving. There is a moment when the arms, hands, and club feel as though they are still moving back while the hips are moving forward. It's just after this moment you want the right elbow to start narrowing the gap between it and the torso. Bringing the right arm closer to the body on the downswing will help you retain the release of your arms and will assist you in swinging down to the ball more from the inside.

Although many believe that you should hold the angle of your arms and wrists as long as possible on the downswing, the general interpretation of this can lead to some costly mistakes in your swing. By over-connecting the right arm you can easily get the club stuck behind you. Trying to retain angles on the downswing can also lead to blocks and even shanks. The grip end of the golf club needs to eventually point towards the center of your body at impact. If you attempt to hold off releasing by over-tucking your right arm, the grip points outside your left hip, leaving the clubface open.

Try this simple drill to help you feel the right arm close to the body on the downswing:

Take a normal backswing but hold it at the top of the swing.

Keeping your back towards the target, tuck your right elbow down and towards the body, then turn your hips slightly towards the target.

Perform this pumping motion several times.

After you get the feel of the pumping motion make a swing down to the ball, ensuring the arms are swinging down to the ball and that the grip end of the club is working towards the center of your body. Remember, arms work up and down. There should be no around in your arm movements.

While working on getting your right arm closer to the body in the downswing remember to create width

on the backswing and allow the right arm to drop while swinging the arms down to the ball. Your power will be created by keeping the club in front of you and by keeping your arms connected in the downswing. Eliminate the concept of retaining the release and use the full power of your body to gain swing speed.

In golf, the right arm close to the body is simply the best way to develop power for your swing.

In Golf Arms Swing in Front of Chest

By swinging with your arms in front of your chest you can eliminate many swing faults associated with controlling your golf club. If your arms get behind you there is a good chance the club will no longer be between your hands and your influence over the golf club will be greatly diminished. To feel the effects of the club not being between the hands and arms grab a golf club, stand straight up and hold it in front of you so that the club is parallel with your spine.

Extend your arms. First, slowly let the club fall to the right in your hands. You will feel a little resistance at first, then more as it falls more quickly. The club feels heavier and heavier. Go back to the start and this time, slowly drop your right elbow. Again, the club feels heavy and it even starts to pull down on the left arm. The arms are no longer in front of you and once this happens your timing and sequence will be affected there on out.

It's much easier to control a light golf club. A lighter golf club can also be swung faster. So, when the club gets heavy it pressures the rest of your body to try to get your arms back in front of you as soon as possible. That's too much action going on during your golf swing! Sometimes it's difficult to pinpoint why exactly the club gets behind you in the swing. If this is the case for you, do this very simple drill:

Hold a 7-iron in one hand and an 8-iron in the other.

Bend over into your address position and position your left arm so it is laying on top of your chest and the clubhead is on the ground.

Place the club in your right-hand directly behind the one in your left-hand.

Swing both clubs back at the same time. Watch them see if either arm allows the club to fall so it's not between the hands and/or the arm falls so they are no longer in front of your chest.

Whichever arm is giving you issues is the one you need to target for improvements.

Here are some elements you need to evaluate if you are having problems controlling the golf club and keeping your arms in front of you:

GRIP-Your left-hand grip should be strong enough that you can set the club swinging back with the left arm only. Otherwise, you will most likely bend your arm to set the club. Your right-hand grip should be positioned so that it can work underneath the club and support it. A very strong right-hand grip will not allow that without the arms getting behind you.

POSTUREToo much knee bend will cause your upper body to stand erect. The arms will be reaching out and not hanging. If you try to support the club with the right-hand from this position

the club will be laid off and the arms will be behind you in the backswing.

LEFT LEG COLLAPSE Your left leg is a stabilizer so if it bends during the backswing, it will change your posture and force your arms behind you. Those are just a few red flags you might want to consider if you are having trouble controlling the club and losing the ability to keep your arms in front of you. A light club allows for a faster and more efficient golf swing so remember, In Golf Arms Swing in Front of Chest.

CHAPTER 14: THE TRIGGER FINGER

L ook at the bottom hand of any good golfer as he grips the club at address and you'll notice a small gap between the index finger and middle finger. In fact, the index finger looks much like it would if squeezing the trigger of a gun.

Hence, the term "trigger finger."

This slight separation may seem minor, but it plays a key role in your ability to control the club. Informing a proper trigger finger position, you give the club a cradle in which to rest at the top of the backswing, preventing the club from wobbling as you transition to the downswing. Keeping a small amount of pressure on the middle joint of the trigger finger improves your feel for the clubhead, too, helping you square the face through impact.

To grip the club correctly with your bottom index finger (right-hand for righties), follow these simple steps:

Assume your regular grip, with your right thumb forming a diagonal line across the handle.

Hook the right index finger around the bottom of the club so that there's about a quarter-inch separating it from the middle finger.

You should see a "V" formed by the right thumb and right fore-finger from the first knuckle to its base.

This configuration will also keep you from placing too much of the handle in your palms. If the right index finger forms a circle from tip to base, around the club, it's a tell-tale sign that you're palming it.

Golf Grip – What is the Trigger Finger?

The success or failure of your golf shots is mostly determined before you even put the club into motion. While that fact is hard for many amateur golfers to understand, it is absolutely true – if you get everything right in terms of your pre-shot setup, you will be well on your way to a positive outcome. You still have to make a quality swing, of course, but most of the hard work will already be completed when you take a good stance and form a good grip. Those might seem like easy points, but few amateur golfers actually get them right on a regular basis. Take the time to create quality pre-shot fundamentals in your game and you will be surprised to see how quickly you can improve.

In this chapter, we are going to look at a seemingly subtle part of the grip. Specifically, we are going to address the 'trigger finger' position that you should form with the pointer finger on your right-hand (for a right-handed golfer). Using a trigger finger grip – meaning your pointer finger is separated slightly from the rest of your fingers as it wraps around the grip – is a great way to add to your feel for the club. There are a number of benefits that come along with using this technique, and really no drawbacks to speak of. As an added bonus, this isn't a position that should take you very long to comfortable with, so you can put it into action and see results almost immediately.

While the grip is a highly personal thing, and there are plenty of different grips that have led to quality ball-striking over the years, there is an argument to be made that all golfers should use the trigger finger. At the very least, you should give this style of grip a try to see if it is able to help improve the consistency of your swing. You want to have control over the golf club at all points during the swing, and the trigger finger might be able to help you toward that goal.

It is often true that the best tips in the game of golf are the simple ones, and they don't come much more simple than the idea of moving your pointer finger slightly down the grip and away from the rest of your fingers. You don't need to understand any complicated swing theory in order to put this tip into action – you can simply adjust the positioning of your finger and start swinging away. Of course, even though this is a simple change, it is not something that should be tested out for the first time on the golf course. Try hitting some shots with a trigger finger grip while on the driving range and take it out to the course after you have had a chance to get comfortable.

All of the content below has been written from the perspective of a right-handed golfer. If you are a left-handed player, please take a moment to reverse the directions as necessary. Obviously, for left-handed players, the trigger finger is going to refer to the pointer finger on the left-hand, as opposed to the right pointer finger for a right-handed player.

Control at the Top

One of the key moments that take place in the golf swing is the transition between the backswing and the downswing. As you change directions at the top, it is easy to lose control of your swing – which can obviously lead to problems when you get back down to the bottom to actually contact the ball. Many amateur golfers allow the club to 'wobble' at the top, which is often the result of a poor grip that doesn't put the fingers in the right position to control the shaft. To correct this problem, you may want to try using the trigger finger grip. Moving your right pointer finger just a bit down the grip will add to the control you have over the club, meaning your swing will be more stable as it transitions from backswing to downswing.

If there are problems present at the top of your swing, those problems can be manifested in a number of different ways when it comes to your ball flight. For instance, allowing the club to drop during the transition will put it under the proper swing plane, leaving you vulnerable for a quick hook or a push out to the right. Or, if you avoid dropping the club inside by pushing it up away from your shoulder, you will end up over the top of the right plane and you will have to attack the ball from the outside. This is the classic slice pattern, although it can also create a pull if your hands are active through the hitting area. Either way, losing control of your swing plane at the top is almost sure to lead to a shot that flies off line significantly.

The best golf swings tend to be those which are controlled more by the body than the hands and arms, which is exactly what will happen in your game when you employ the trigger finger grip. Believe it or not, making this adjustment in your grip is a great way to quiet the action of your hands during the swing. You will have a greater degree of control over the club with this kind of grip, meaning the club won't be so quick to respond to subtle moves in your hands and wrists. Now that the club is steadier throughout the swing, you can focus on using the rotation of your body to propel the club through the hitting area. This is a powerful way to play the game, and you are likely to find that you quickly fall in love with how solid your swing feels while putting the trigger finger to use.

Getting back to the topic of the top of the swing, another benefit of the trigger finger grip is avoiding the extra-long backswing that dooms the swing of so many amateur players. The average golfer thinks they need to make a long swing in order to hit powerful shots, but going too far in this effort is only going to harm your swing in the end. You want to make a full shoulder rotation, but adding length to your arm swing at the top will make it difficult to strike the ball cleanly. By using the trigger finger, you will be giving the club a place to 'rest' at the top, and you will be less inclined to swing too far beyond an appropriate backswing length. Use your rotation to form a full backswing while you keep your hands steady to make sure the club stops right around the parallel position at the top.

Controlling the club at the top of the swing should be one of your top motivations for using the trigger finger grip. After only a few practice swings, you should begin to notice the difference in the way the club is transitioning at the top, assuming you have been using a grip that did not feature a trigger finger position. You will now be able to use your lower body more aggressively in the downswing, which is exactly what you should be doing in order to generate power through the hitting area. It can be hard to believe that such a small change can make such an important difference in your swing but don't dismiss this idea until you have tried it for yourself.

Stability Through the Hit

One of the important parts of the golf swing that doesn't get talked about often enough is the ability to keep the club stable through the hitting area. Any way you look at it, the moment of impact is a violent collision between the clubhead and the ball. Powerful players can swing the club through impact at more than 100 miles per hour, which is obviously more than enough force to create quite a bit of energy when the collision occurs. While you would love to have each and every impact with the ball come right off the middle of the clubface, that obviously isn't going to happen. You are going to miss-hit the majority of your shots, so your ability to hold the face stable when that happens will have a lot to do with how you score.

There are a number of factors that contribute to your ability to hold the face steady at impact. One is the strength that you have in your hands and forearms.

Players with plenty of strength in the small muscles of the hands and forearms generally have an easier time holding the face steady. This strength pays off on all shots, but it really comes in handy when playing out of the rough. The long grass found in the rough wants to stop and twist the club, and it takes plenty of strength to fight off those forces.

Another factor in this equation is the grip that you choose to use on the club, which is where the trigger finger comes into the picture. By using a trigger finger positioning on the grip, you are effectively spreading out your right-hand – meaning you are covering more of the grip with your hand. In turn, you will be able to hold the club in a steadier position through impact due to the fact that you have more of the club directly under your control. It will be harder for the clubhead to twist simply because your hands will have an added degree of security on the grip. This is another point that might seem subtle and small, but it can pay off in a big way when you are able to carve the ball out of the rough while keeping the face square to your target.

Once you are able to put the trigger finger to use in your game, and you start to feel an increased sense of control at impact as a result, you will love the way your confidence grows on all different kinds of shots around the course. It is a great feeling to know that you are going to be able to hold the club steady through the hit, as this is not a feeling that most players are able to enjoy – and you may have not felt it previously during your golf career. You will find that more of your shots start to fly on the line once you make this adjustment, and those shots will also hold their line better once in the air. Simply put, you should be a better ball-striker due to adding a trigger finger to your grip.

Other Key Grip Points

Yes – using the trigger finger position can be tremendously helpful in the way your grip works during the swing. However, it is not the only point that needs to be considered while putting together your grip. In fact, you can still get the grip quite wrong despite the presence of a trigger finger if you fail to hit on the other key fundamentals. With that in mind, it is important to highlight some of the other points that you should be watching for in your swing beyond the trigger finger. Make sure you are hitting on all of the points below when forming your grip and you will be on the right track.

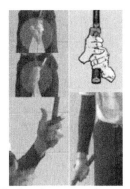

Soft grip pressure. This is the number one key when it comes to the grip that you use in your golf game. Squeezing the grip too tightly is an extremely common problem, and it makes it difficult to swing the club freely through the hitting area. If you are struggling to create power and consistency in your swing, checking on your grip pressure is one of the first things you should do. Proper grip pressure is actually quite simple, despite the fact that many golfers get it wrong.

Your goal should be to use a grip that is just tight enough to allow you to keep control over the club, and no tighter. You obviously need to control the club through the hitting area – and you certainly don't want the club to go flying out of your hands at any time – but you don't want to hang on so tight that the club is not allowed to move freely. Practice using a soft grip pressure while working on your short game and gradually move into longer and longer swings until you are comfortable hitting your driver while squeezing the grip just the right amount.

Fingers, not palm. When placed in your hands, the grip of the club should be running along the base of your fingers, rather than running up into your palm. Putting the grip into the palm of the hands is a classic beginner's mistake, and the result is a swing that looks stiff and uncomfortable. You need to be able to engage your hands and wrists in the swing in order to generate speed, but that will be nearly impossible when you put the grip into your palm. By putting the handle of the club into your palms, you will be 'locking up' your wrists, and you will have a hard time making a free swing as a result.

This is one of those points in the game of golf that is not up for debate. There are plenty of unique and individual aspects to golf swings even at the highest levels of the game, but you aren't going to see any pro players swinging the club with the handle in their palms. Keep the club down near the base of your fingers and enjoy the freedom that this type of grip provides.

Find the right grip strength. In golf, grip strength refers not to how tightly you hold on to the handle, but rather to the position of your left-hand. A strong grip is one that has the left-hand turned significantly to the right at address, while a weak grip is just the opposite. If you can see more than two knuckles on the back of your left-hand at address, you are using a strong grip.

If you can see two or fewer knuckles, your grip would be placed in the weak category. You can play good golf by going in either direction, but you need to be sure that you are using a grip that compliments the other techniques in your game. Experiment with both kinds of grips until you settle on one that is just right for you.

Friction is crucial. Trying to swing a club without having a good grip on the handle is a pursuit that is destined to fail. In other words, you need to make sure that your equipment is providing you with the chance to form a solid grip on the club – a grip that will not slip during the swinging action. To reach this goal, you first need to make sure you have quality grips on your clubs, and you need to keep those grips in good condition.

Clean your grips regularly, and replace them when they start to get hard and slick. Also, you may want to consider using a golf glove while you play, if you don't use on already. A glove is a relatively inexpensive piece of gear that can make it far easier to grip the club, especially if your hands tend to sweat, or if you play in the rain.

The importance of a good grip simply cannot be overstated. If you are able to form a good grip on the club prior to each swing, your game will have a far better chance to succeed than if you were using a poor grip. Use the points listed above, along with the trigger finger position which we have been discussing, to create the best grip of your golfing life.

Trigger Finger in the Short Game

Another benefit of using the trigger finger in your golf grip is the fact that this is a fundamental which translates beautifully into the short game. The short game, as you should already know, is extremely important to your ability to score well on the golf course. By keeping things consistent from your long game to the short game, you should find that your overall performance improves in all facets. You won't need to dramatically change your grip as you get closer to the green because the trigger finger will help you to play quality short shots just as it helps you in the full swing.

It is the stability of this kind of grip which really allows it to shine in the short game. You want the club to be moving in a predictable manner while playing short shots, and it will do just that when you use a trigger finger. Since your hands will have tremendous control over the club as it swings, you will be able to focus on using the movement of your shoulders and arms to send the ball accurately toward the target. This grip can be used for all of the different shots that you face on and around the greens – putts, chip shots, pitch shots, bunker shots, and more. No matter what kind of shot it is, you are almost certain to love the way your short game feels with the trigger finger grip in place.

This is a topic that certainly doesn't seem like it could be that important in the grand scheme of the game as a whole. Don't be deceived by the relatively minor profile of this grip change, as it can have a major impact on how you play the game. Take some time during an upcoming practice session to experiment with the trigger finger grip and you may find that you want to immediately make it a part of your permanent grip technique. Good luck!

CHAPTER 15: SOUND POSTURE

Poor posture in your everyday activities – walking, working, driving the car – can cause unwanted side effects. So can poor posture when addressing the golf ball.

If you setup without the knees, hips, and back flexed and tilted properly, you short-circuit the swing right from the start. Without good posture, it's difficult to rotate the upper and lower body, maintain good balance, and achieve a consistent swing plane. The result: bad ball-striking.

Just as carrying yourself with good posture presents a positive image in everyday situations, sound posture on the course is rooted in a proud appearance – standing tall, with an open chest and straight spine. In other words, a look (and feeling) that says, "Bring it on."

Follow these steps to a perfect pre-swing posture:

Addressing the ball, stand upright with your feet shoulder-width apart (insteps aligned with outsides of shoulders).

Pull your shoulders back with your head held high, as though standing at attention.

Grip the club in your usual manner and hold it in front of you, horizontally, with the butt end pointing at your belly button and your elbows close to your sides.

Bend slightly at the knees, with your balance spread evenly between the heels and balls of your feet. Your backside should stick out a little to keep the spine lined up nicely.

Tilt forward from the hips – not the waist – letting the club fall naturally downward with the clubhead on the ground.

Make sure your head does not bow downward, and that you maintain the position of your shoulders and spine.

If the clubhead is not directly behind the ball as you complete the process, simply step forward or back as needed to place it there. Don't bend or slump forward with the back or waist, don't stand up straighter, and don't push or pull the club into place with the arms. Maintain your posture and change the club's position by moving the feet only.

Adjust the width of your feet based on the club you're hitting (wider for longer clubs, narrower for shorter clubs).

Good Posture for Good Golf

If you spend most of your golf practice time working on complicated moves and advanced swing theories, you certainly aren't alone. Most golfers spend their time at the driving range trying to figure out detailed ways to move the club around their body in order to strike solid shots. After all, golf is a hard game, so the solution to your troubles on the course must be pretty complicated, right? No – not necessarily. In fact, it is far more likely that your game will improve as a result of working on the basics than if you allow yourself to get caught up in complex theories and techniques. Keeping it simple is the best way to play good golf, and one of the simple keys to this game is playing from a solid posture.

Sure, it is true that working on your posture isn't the most exciting thing that you can do at the golf course. Perfecting this specific part of your technique is rather boring, to be honest, but it is incredibly important nonetheless. If you manage to master a great stance that puts you in a quality position over the ball shot after shot, you will stand a great chance to improve the level of your play in short order. Many golfers make the mistake of thinking that posture isn't particularly important, but nothing could be further from the truth-finding good posture at address, and then holding that posture throughout the swing, is one of the biggest keys to high-level ball-striking.

Teaching golf posture can be a bit of a tricky proposition because of the individual nature of the stance. Each golfer has his or her own stance that is unique in one way or another – and that is just fine. You don't need to copy the stance of any other golfer precisely in order to have success. However, you do need to hit on certain basic fundamentals if you are going to set yourself up for a positive outcome at the end of your swing. Looking at the postures and stances that you see on the PGA Tour is a great example of this concept. While each player will have a characteristic or two that sets their stance apart from the crowd, most will still fall in line with a number of key fundamental points.

In this chapter, we are going to walk through some of the most important points related to the posture that you use in your stance. Simply by understanding why posture is important and which keys you should focus on, you can improve your game in short order. One of the nice things about working on this part of your game is the fact that improvement can come quicker than it does when trying to make other changes. Take a step forward with your posture today and there is a good chance you will start playing better within your next couple of rounds.

All of the content below is based on a right-handed golfer. If you happen to play left-handed, please take a moment to reverse the directions as necessary.

Why Does It Matter?

Before you head out to work hard on improving your posture, it makes sense to have a good understanding of just why this point is so crucial in the first place. You are more likely to remain motivated to work on your posture when you actually understand why it matters – without this information, you may be tempted to just give up and work on other points. So, take a few moments to read through this section and fill yourself with all the motivation needed to take on the task of building a better posture.

Following is a list of three points that highlight the importance of using an excellent posture as you swing the golf club.

Maintaining your level. One of the biggest challenges in the game of golf is correctly locating the bottom of your swing on each and every shot. Particularly when hitting irons directly off of the turf, you have to locate the bottom of your swing just past the golf ball if you are going to make clean contact. That task is challenging enough on its own, but it becomes almost impossible without great posture.

If you have poor posture in your swing, you will move up and down as the swing develops, meaning you will have almost no chance to find the bottom of your swing successfully. On the other hand, great posture keeps your body steady and prevents you from going up and down for no reason. The result? Your swing arc is more predictable, and the club bottoms out in the same spot time after time. There is certainly more to good ball-striking than just maintaining your level in the swing, but this is a key point that you can't afford to get wrong.

Enable a great turn. You probably already know that a great turn is one of the keys to producing power in your golf swing. However, did you know that you will struggle to make a good turn if you don't have your posture under control? It's true – making a full shoulder turn going back and hip turn going forward is almost impossible without the right posture to support your rotation. If you feel like you struggle to turn sufficiently in the swing, it might not be your flexibility that is the problem – instead, it could be something as simple as a poor posture preventing you from reaching your power potential.

Engage your lower body. When you set yourself into a solid stance and posture, there is a good chance that you are going to engage your lower body as a result – and that is good news. The lower body has a great deal to do with quality ball-striking, yet many amateur golfers fail to get their legs involved at any point during the swing. You will likely be amazed at the power and consistency that you can bring to your swing through the use of your legs, and it all starts by building a solid posture. Nearly every pro golfer in the world does a great job of using his or her lower body to create speed and stability, and you should be following that lead with your own game.

In reality, there are actually plenty of other benefits to using a good posture beyond these three points. However, the importance of these points should be more than enough to convince you to work on this part of your game. Once you get started with your first range session, it should quickly become clear to you just how much improvement can be made through the process of building a great posture and stance over the ball.

The Key Fundamentals

At this point, you should have a clear understanding of why it is that you need to use a great posture during your swing. However, you still need to learn what it is that makes up a good posture in the first place. In this section, we are going to touch on the points that make up a posture that can be relied on for consistent performance swing after swing. If you are able to include all of the following points in your posture with each club in your bag, the performance of your game is sure to take a big step forward.

Flat back. This is perhaps the single-most-important fundamentals within the posture. If you are going to stand properly over the ball, you need to have your back in a relatively flat position from your waist all the way up into your neck. This position is key because it is going to permit you to make a great turn with ease. When you hunch over in your back, it becomes difficult – if not impossible – to rotate nicely away from the ball. Focus on keeping your back in a flat position from the time you take your stance until well after the ball has been struck.

Chin up. As far as the posture goes, this might be the point that is missed more than any other. When you take your stance, it is important that you keep your chin up and away from your chest – despite the fact that you might think this advice runs contrary to the concept of keeping your head down. The idea of keeping your head down is one of the oldest tips in the game, but it just isn't very accurate when you think carefully about what you have to do in the swing.

To make a good golf swing, you need a big shoulder turn away from the ball – and keeping your head and chin down is going to prevent you from making that turn. When your chin is down, it will physically be in the way of your left shoulder as it tries to rotate back. To make sure there is nothing in the way of a great turn, keep your chin up while maintaining eye contact with the ball.

Flexed knees. You might think first about your upper body when you consider posture, but the lower body is just as important in the big picture of how you stand over the ball. You need to sink into your lower body by adding a fair amount of knee flex to your stance at address. Knee flex will not only engage your legs in the swing right from the start, but it will also give you a stable platform on which to build your swing. Far too many amateur golfers stand with their knees straight as they get the swing started, and the lower body is never able to get involved in the action as a result. You don't have to get into a deep squat or anything like that in order to find a good posture, but it is important to make sure your knees are at least moderately flexed before the swing begins.

Properly balanced. You might not think of balance as being part of the posture equation, but it really does fit in this category because it relates to how your body is positioned before the swing. At address, you don't want to feel like you are leaning in any one direction – rather, you should be comfortably balanced right in the middle of your feet. To highlight this point, you can ask a friend to come up and gently push against one of your shoulders while you are in your stance. If you have good balance and posture, you will have no trouble 'holding your ground'. However, if there is trouble with your balance, you may find that you quickly have to come out of your stance to avoid falling over.

In the end, finding good posture is actually fairly simple. With a flat back, your chin up, your knees flexed, and your balance under control, you will be ready to go. Of course, the challenge does not stop there as it relates to posture. Not only do you need to start out your swing with great posture, but you need to keep that posture throughout the rest of the swing. So, in the next section, we are going to look at some points which relate directly to the task of keeping your posture in place while the swing develops around you.

Taking Advantage of Your Posture

Okay – so now you are in a good posture before you swing the club, that's the end of it, right? It should all be smooth sailing from this point forward? Not so fast. Yes, getting into a good posture before the swing is important, but you still have plenty of work to do before you can watch the ball sail beautifully toward the target.

You need to know to find a way to take advantage of the posture you have created, meaning you have to hold that posture to the best of your ability throughout the impending swing. To highlight the key points on this topic, we have created another list below. This one includes all of the fundamentals involved in holding on to your posture successfully. Hit on these points and there is little doubt that you will be going in the right direction.

Watch the right knee. If your posture is going to fall apart during your swing, that issue will usually start with the right knee. As the club swings back, it is tempting to allow your right knee to straighten up. When that happens, you may allow your entire body to straighten up, which would cause you to lose your posture shortly after the swing began. To avoid this problem, pay close attention to the action of your right knee as you hit some practice shots. Ideally, you will be able to keep your right knee stable and flexed throughout the backswing and into the downswing. It is okay if you allow just a bit of movement in that knee in order to promote rhythm and tempo, but it should not come all the way up into a straight position.

Don't over-swing. One of the biggest issues that come up with regard to amateur golfers losing their posture is the problem of over-swinging. When you over-swing – or allow your swing to go farther back than necessary – you run the risk of both losing your balance and pulling yourself up out of your posture. If you are trying too hard to move the club as far back as possible, it is very likely that you will come up and out of your stance before you ever have a chance to complete your transition and head into the downswing.

There is nothing good that can be said about over-swinging, as you aren't actually going to gain any clubhead speed through this kind of technique. Keep your backswing tight and controlled at all times, making sure to change direction while you are still on balance and down in your posture. Those who are used to making a swing that is too long may find that this is a difficult habit to break, but it is important enough to focus on in practice sessions until it has been corrected.

Use your lower body aggressively. There are many differences between the swings of professional golfers and the average amateur player, but one of the biggest contrasts is the way the lower body is used. The average pro uses his or her lower body aggressively right from the top of the downswing. The average amateur? Not so much. Unfortunately, the average amateur player struggles to engage their lower body in the swing, and they lack power as a result. Now that you are in a good stance, you should be able to use your lower body better right from the top of the swing to build speed that can be carried all the way through impact. Work on turning your left hip open to the target as soon as the downswing begins and you will find that you are able to create more speed than ever before.

It would be a shame to work hard on building a great posture only to let it go to waste. Once you have learned how to create a solid posture at address, use the points on this list to make sure you aren't wasting that posture after the club goes in motion. Only when you combine a great starting posture with a solid in-swing technique will you be able to reap the rewards you desire.

Putting and Posture

The importance of posture doesn't end when you put down your full swing clubs and pick up your putter. As you might imagine, the topic of posture remains extremely important with regard to putting, although the fundamentals are going to change a bit. When putting, you don't need to make a big shoulder turn, so some of the points that are key when making a full swing won't really be relevant in this conversation. Specifically, if you feel most comfortable with your chin down into your chest while making a putting stroke, go for it – that position isn't going to stop you from rolling the ball nicely.

Also, you can afford to be a bit 'hunched over' at address while preparing to putt without doing any harm to your game. This is a point of personal preference – some golfers like to stay in a flat back position, while others want to relax and hunch a bit to feel like they are getting down into the stroke. Either way is fine, so go with whatever feels most natural to you. Of course, you can easily test out different postures on the putting green, so experiment with a variety of positions until you settle on one that seems to perform at a high level.

One point that does stay the same between your putting posture and your full swing stance is the issue of balance. No matter what kind of shot you are hitting around the golf course, you always need to be as balanced as possible. When setting up to putt, make sure your weight is evenly distributed between your feet to promote a stroke that swings back and through with no issues at all. Poor balance is one of the leading causes of poor performance on the putting green, so be sure to check on this point as you are working through the process of settling on a specific posture for your putting stroke.

Posture might not be the most exciting topic in the game of golf, but it certainly is one of the most important when it comes to determining your score. If you can stand over the ball in a manner that gives your body a chance to move in the correct manner throughout the swing, hitting the ball solidly will become a much easier task. It is often the basics in golf that turn out to be the most important points, so don't make the mistake of overlooking the critical nature of the posture when it comes to improving your game.

THANKS

We hope this no-fluff golf book will help your game, and here at Thomas Golf we never tire of helping golfers out.

We appreciate you reading **The Key Principles VOL 31** and enjoy the game.

.

Printed in Great Britain
by Amazon

82145505R00102